CEAUCESCU'S CHILDREN

To Vonnie and Michael
with love from Joan

CEAUCESCU'S CHILDREN

The Amazing Story of One Woman's
Mission to Romanian Orphans

JOAN SIMKINS

Marshall Pickering
An Imprint of HarperCollins*Publishers*

Marshall Pickering is an Imprint of
HarperCollins*Religious*
Part of HarperCollins*Publishers*
77-85 Fulham Palace Road, London W6 8JB

First published in Great Britain in 1998 by HarperCollins*Religious*
1 3 5 7 9 10 8 6 4 2

A catalogue record for this book
is available from the British Library.

ISBN 0 551 03126 3

Printed and bound in Great Britain by
Caledonian International Book Manufacturing Ltd, Glasgow

Dedicated to the children of the White Cross Mission
orphanages in Bratca and Remeti, Romania.

*Gotheffio than flehas vean tha Doaz tha ve, ha na wrewh
go defendya angye, rag a rima ew an wlascore a Thew.*
'Suffer the little children to come unto me, and forbid
them not, for of such is the kingdom of God.'
(Luke 18:16, AV)

OUT OF THE DARKNESS, INTO THE LIGHT
A CANDLE OF HOPE

Sad eyes look through me,
Please see me,
See the light I bring to you.

You listen to what I say,
But do you hear me?
Hear the words of hope.

Tiny hands touch me,
Cold and searching.
Feel the warmth of my loving arms.

Your mind tortures you,
Learn to love yourself,
You are special.

Leave the world of darkness behind,
Step forward into a new dream.

ROB WILDE, VOLUNTEER (BRATCA)
FEBRUARY 1996

Contents

Acknowledgements

I am grateful to those hundreds of people whose actions, prayers and feelings have in fact written the inspiring story of the White Cross Mission. Echoing the words of one volunteer, everyone – Pat and the Directors, every volunteer, the coordinators, the managers, the secretary, the Friends Groups, the sponsors, the fundraisers – every single person who has contributed anything at all has given something valuable. They have contributed also in supplying the material for this book.

I owe particular gratitude to those who, by talking or writing, have given firsthand descriptions of their experiences. I have relied on Pat's accounts of some of the children and volunteers, and on her regular letters to supporters, which are an excellent record of the story of the Mission so far and its hopes for the future.

I thank Graham Banks and Jeff and Jenny Townsend for meeting me and supplying me with information and background. Thank you, too, to Sue for transforming my badly typed script into a respectable one.

I thank all the volunteers who have been willing to meet me, for describing their experiences and feelings, and for talking so frankly. I thank those volunteers whose articles and poems are included. They add a fresh and authentic perspective, painting pictures which bring the whole venture to life in a way that nothing else could.

I would like to pay special tribute to Alan Woodburn, who generously gave me access to his unpublished manuscript and allowed me to quote from it. Also to Kay Toms, who was happy that I should quote from her booklet. Thank you too, Kay, for those vital black files which contain a chronological record of everything written about the White Cross, including newpaper articles and letters to supporters. They have been my only textbook.

Thank you to Richard Gendall of the *Teere ha Tavas* for taking the trouble to translate the words of Jesus, 'Suffer the little children to come unto me, and forbid them not, for of such is the kingdom of God,' into Cornish for me.

Thank you to my stepson Bill Simkins for his interest in this book, and for his willingness to listen when I thought aloud at times – for when one is writing a book it is always on one's mind. Thank you, Bill, for on occasion supplying *le mot* – and sometimes 'le phrase' – *juste*.

Finally, I am indebted to Kate Davies for her enthusiasm and encouragement, and to Bryony Benier for her thorough and meticulous editing of the script.

Foreword

Mama Pat has become something of a legend in Romania, as I discovered personally when I made a recent visit to see for myself something of the work of the White Cross Mission, established by Pat Robson and continuing to do impressive work for Romania's children.

I was able to see and experience at first hand the fruit of Pat's labours – two small houses where children previously abandoned to an orphanage are once again enjoying life and flourishing as members of a village family, each house surrounded with a small-holding for fruit and vegetables. The transformation in the children is plainly evident – now they have real hope for the future.

The White Cross Mission continues its search for such houses; indeed, I saw two further places where already negotiations were well on the way, where more children can be housed, clothed and fed.

But there is more – a whole lot more – which the White Cross Mission and its numerous volunteers, young and old, have accomplished by way of transformation. Their work, though focused on orphaned and abandoned children, has had a considerable effect in the wider communities in which they have worked. While bringing huge improvements in so many practical ways, they have also been able to influence for good the relationships and well-being of the communities where they have been – a truly Christian work where, in the Saviour's words, 'In as much as you have done it to the least of these, you have done it to me'.

Mama Pat and the work of the White Cross Mission deserve continued and increased support for this compelling work of mercy and love undertaken in Christ's name. Having seen for myself, I returned home both encouraged and challenged; encouraged that so much is being accomplished by so few, and challenged to see to it that the work is increased and enlarged – for the sake of the children.

David Ebor
Archbishop of York

Introduction

One day I walked into a charity shop in Truro and noticed, mounted on cards, several photos of dark-haired children. Beneath each photo were a few sentences about the child. I was intrigued: this was my first encounter with the White Cross Mission. The lady in the shop explained that it was a charity which aimed to help some of the children who had been found, in terrible conditions, in Romanian orphanages at the end of Ceaucescu's dictatorship.

I returned to the shop. I wanted to help. One day when I went in I met Jahal de Meritens, who told me of some of his experiences with the Mission. He suggested that I might start a support group in my local area. I felt I could not only sympathize, but also identify wholeheartedly with the spirit and intentions of this group of people who were doing their best to rescue children from a dark future.

Two things about the White Cross Mission amaze and touch me. The first is the very special feeling which those abandoned children evoke in those who go out to care for them. The children are so desperate for affection and so overjoyed to receive it. It sets them alight with a kind of new life and this returns to those who give them love. It is reassuring to find so much warmth and genuine goodness in the hearts of so many – mainly young – persons who have gone out to Romania. The second is Pat Robson. Whether her unusual compassion and character stem from her genetic inheritance, her upbringing and environment or her surrender to the teaching and spirit of Jesus, she is a woman of whom the human race can be proud. Her story, and that of the White Cross, should be told.

1

Ceaucescu's legacy

December 1989. A revolution in Romania finally exposes to the world the darkness of a regime which has left indelible scars on a country and a people. Those most hurt by the years of despotic madness are the forgotten children. Locked away in lightless, filthy orphanages, they were unloved, unwanted: 'Ceaucescu's children'.

Easter 1991. A convoy of assorted vehicles from Cornwall makes its way across Europe, laden with food and clothes. Led by Pat Robson, the convoy was carrying more than just material goods. It carried hope, love and above all a determination, felt by all those involved, to bring light and life to Ceaucescu's forgotten children. Pat Robson tells the story:

> The first convoy consisted of eight vehicles. We stuck a Cornish flag on each of them for no real reason except that we needed to identify each other. The flags were high enough up for us to be able to see each other as we went across

Europe. We had all the borders to get through with our loads and it took ages. As one lorry went through it pulled in and waited for the others. It was a slow old business. We got to the Austro-Hungarian border and there was a little man there with sheaves of papers and I can well remember Mike, Cornwall's biggest policeman; a huge guy he is. He said, 'Oh I've had enough of this', and he elbowed his way to the front of the line. He towered over this little guy, jabbed his thumb at the papers and said, 'Now look here mate, we don't need all this bumf.' He was wearing a Cornish flag on his flak jacket and he said, 'We're the WHITE CROSS', and this little man looked up and wrote 'THE WHITE CROSS' on the top line and said, 'And who is your employer?' Mike drew himself up to his six foot whatever, stuck his finger in the air and said, 'GOD of course mate. G-O-D GOD!' Luckily for us the little man had a good sense of humour. He stood up, saluted us and waved us through. We looked in amazement at each other and said, 'Well from now on we're THE WHITE CROSS'.

Before we left England we had already chosen our motto – 'It is better to light a candle than to curse the darkness.' When we arrived in Romania and found the darkness and the suspicion and the Securitate it looked – and felt – so much, well almost as if the candle was ready to be blown out. Because we'd gone with all this good feeling and weren't welcomed. We were met by sullen frightened people. I felt like kissing the ground Popestyle when we left because we were so relieved to get out. When we talked about the White Cross going into the dark and bringing light into the darkness we felt that was so much what we had been trying to do that first trip.

This is how the flag of Cornwall – a white cross on a black background – used first merely as a sign of recognition, proved to be an apt and meaningful symbol of the mission to Romania which Pat had initiated. The flag had traditionally stood not only for the silver of tin coming out of the black ore but also for the light of the gospel shining in the darkness. Mike was right when he said that their employer was God, although Pat was perhaps more immediately in command.

Millions throughout the world must have read about or seen pictures of the plight of 'Ceaucescu's children', once the news hit the headlines. Many people no doubt felt frustrated and impotent in the face of such appalling, heartless tragedy. Many were also galvanized into action. The BBC film *Ceaucescu's Children*, shown just before Easter 1990, had an enormous impact. Individuals and groups wanting to send aid or to go out and help sprang up all over

Europe, and even further afield. Pat Robson, a Diocesan Youth Officer in Cornwall, was one of these individuals.

Born during the Second World War, Pat enjoyed an idyllic, gentle childhood, wanting for nothing, saying her daily prayers without question as a matter of habit. God became a living reality for her while she was preparing for confirmation at the age of fourteen, when a quiet and gentle priest told her this:

> Every evening go into your room alone. Take two chairs facing each other. Sit down on one and imagine that Jesus is sitting on the other. Just talk to him; have a silent conversation with him about everything you feel and you need to say, to ask, everything in your mind.

It was at this time of preparation that Pat received a clear call to preach. She started a Bible class (with more enthusiasm than understanding, as she says now!) and specialized in Religious Education at school.

She trained as a teacher and 1964 saw her teaching in East Africa, where she met and married a white South African. She gave birth to one child, Philip, in Kenya and with a lifelong love of children and young people, she longed for more children of her own. Sadly, it was not to be and she suffered eleven miscarriages. The only option was to have a hysterectomy.

The following years brought many changes for Pat. The family moved to Aldington in Kent in 1970 and in 1971 Mark, a two-year-old Barnardo boy, was adopted. Then they moved first to Devon, and later to Newcastle, but in 1973 the marriage broke up. Pat, with Philip and Mark, decided to live in Cornwall. Why Cornwall? Pat had had a holiday there just once. When considering where to make a new and permanent home she first thought of the Lake District, but perhaps in memory of that holiday, Cornwall, equally beautiful and romantic but very different, was the final choice. She had probably not heard then of the white cross on a black background, originally the flag of St Piran who became the patron saint of Cornwall and, according to an old legend, was supposed to have discovered the first tin.

Pat settled down with Philip and Mark in a little house in Mousehole and Pat, to her amusement as well as chagrin, read one day in a local paper the headline 'FIRST WOMAN IN MOUSEHOLE TO BE DIVORCED'. At first she earned their livelihood by painting, a gift she had inherited from her mother. She soon discovered the sort of pictures which would sell well, but had time to paint others, more pleasing to herself.

In 1974 she restarted her teaching career at Sir Humphry Davy Grammar School for Boys. In 1985 she became a Lay Reader for the Church of England and began to think about ordination as Deacon with the hope of becoming a priest. She was ordained as Deacon in June 1987 and in September of that year became Diocesan Youth Officer. She and the family moved to live in Truro, where her job was based. She started City Kids, an organization which arranged holidays in Cornwall for children living in cities who would otherwise be deprived of such joys. All was running smoothly when, out of the blue, came another test of faith.

Almost immediately after moving to Truro, Pat became unwell. Friends, and Pat herself, wondered if this was due to stress from all the recent changes in her life. Probably her GP thought this too, for though she went to see him in October 1987, she was not referred to a specialist until February of the following year. After the examination the consultant told her not to return home as he needed to operate immediately. However, she insisted that she must go home for one night as she had children and dogs to look after. So the operation was delayed by one day. After it, the surgeon gave her the good news that the surgery had been successful. One day later, however, and she might have died as the cancer was fast growing and had threatened to eat into her liver.

Although her life had been saved, Pat was in a low state physically and it would have been easy to give in mentally and spiritually. But as she began to recover, her strength and enthusiasm for life returned. Six months after the operation she became guardian to three West Indian children whose mother was dying and who had bequeathed them to Pat in her will. The family had been living in Birmingham and Pat knew the children through the City Kids holidays. The eldest, a girl called Yolanda, joined the family in September 1988, and when their mother died in December her two brothers Ras and David came too.

The early months of 1989 saw Pat and her extended family settling into a busy, contented life in Truro. But as 1989 drew to a close and the new decade began, the traumatic pictures of abandoned children which emerged from a Romania in turmoil shocked Pat into action.

A Social Services team from Cornwall returned from Romania in August 1990 after a short visit to some of the orphanages, and when Pat heard Margaret Craven, one of the team's members, describe some of the horrific things she had seen, she at once said, 'We can't just sit here; we must do something.'

The next day she was at Diocesan House discussing plans with her secretary. 'I could sell my car, buy a van, fill it up with things, and then we could drive across Europe and see for ourselves ...' At that moment Quinten Wyvern-Batt came bounding up the stairs. The office door was open.

'What are you girls talking about?' They told him and his reaction was swift. 'Well, if you go I'll pay for the trip.' From that moment it was on.

Pat immediately wrote to all the Church Youth Groups, to the Brownies, Cubs, Scouts and Guides, and to every school in Cornwall to announce that she was planning a trip to Romania to help the children in the orphanages, and to ask if they could send anything which they thought might be helpful, particularly soap. The response taught her that if you need help, involve children. She was delighted. Schools phoned up from all over Cornwall, asking, 'Where shall we deliver?' The first thing she had to do was provide a warehouse for all the donated goods.

Then offers of practical help also started to flood in. 'I'd like to come with you.' And Pat had to enquire, 'Do you have a vehicle? Can you pay for it?' The phone hardly stopped ringing during the first few weeks. She had started an avalanche of good will, and it was a bit scary though immensely exciting as the momentum began to increase. The warehouse was so full it was in danger of bursting, and soon she had been offered the use of eight vehicles and between £30,000 and £40,000 in cash.

Pat realized that to lead a group of eight vans and twenty-four people across Europe, not knowing where they were going or exactly what lay ahead, would be totally irresponsible. She would go first herself. So she went to see Margaret, who knew something of Romania from her first visit with the Social Services. 'Please come with me and show me one or two of the places you saw when you went with the group.'

In January 1991, using some of the money which had been contributed by Mr Wyvern-Batt, Pat and Margaret flew to Bucharest. Immediately on arrival, Pat experienced for the first time that darkness with which she was to become so familiar. The city which had once been called 'The Paris of the East' was a grey, grim place. The airport was manned by soldiers armed with machine guns; the luggage conveyor belt was not working; neither were the electric lights – or they were not turned on. Many planes were delayed, and people were standing around looking tired and colourless. As they drove through the city, bumping over the potholes, they could only just see ghostlike people sitting in their cars. There were no lights. Everywhere there was gloom and darkness.

Pat and Margaret flew on to Cluj-Napoca to visit the headquarters of the German Red Cross who were in charge of that area of Western Romania. They found the headquarters in a hotel. The facade and foyer were pleasant but inside it was dark and ominous. There were no lights and no rods on the stair carpet, so ascending was rather treacherous. They eventually found the suite of rooms which housed the Red Cross offices – teeming with Germans who seemed completely uninterested in them.

They had wanted to say quite simply, 'Look, we've got money and we want to help, but we don't want to do anything uncoordinated; we want to be part of what you're doing. We'll do anything we can to help.'

Sadly, the Germans just didn't seem to take any notice of this concrete offer of help. Was it that they considered the British rather disorganized – coming across with their small vans (a bit like the Dunkirk flotillas) held together with string and breaking down here and there? The German organization was certainly sophisticated. Pat and Margaret felt that perhaps in contrast they did appear too amateurish.

Nonetheless, they stayed in the same room for four or five hours feeling ignored and redundant. Then one man announced in German that he was just going to a place called Remeti where a new consignment of sixty children had arrived from Cadea. It seemed a casual remark – made as he was leaving – but it turned out to be providential and of dramatic consequence for Pat's mission.

'Can we come with you?' Pat said. There was some humming and hawing, but finally the answer was 'Yes', perhaps, Pat thought, because they were glad to say 'Auf Wiedersehen' to the English ladies.

The journey from Cluj to Remeti was long and tiring, but as they drove up into the mountains, the air was crisp and the sun shone. The views were spectacularly beautiful as the valley opened up into the village at the top. They were confronted by a gaunt-looking hospital surrounded by wire fencing. They drove in. There was no sign of any children, but they could hear a strange wailing that did not sound human. The travellers were greeted by the village doctor. He spoke good English but poor German and was complaining about the disinfectant that the Germans had brought with them.

'I have no water, I've got sixty children and I've not enough food.' Because his English was fluent, he was happy talking to Pat and Margaret and he introduced them to some of the children. They were taken aback. It was only three days since the children had come from Cadea, where their heads had been shaved. They were of varying ages, from about seven to fourteen, but most of them were unable to stand or walk and were just penned in their cots.

Pat's first impressions of Remeti were of children rocking backwards and forwards, wide, staring eyes, useless limbs flailing about, and that strange keening noise, like an animal wail. The noise was not loud but it impinged on Pat's consciousness. The smell in the rooms was not too good, but the place did look reasonably clean.

The doctor then took them downstairs, where the children who could walk were standing around. Each of the rooms downstairs was about ten feet by twelve feet and housed fifteen children, but was otherwise empty, apart from two Romanian staff who were doing their best to look after them. This seemed to be a pretty hopeless task, as there was nothing for the children to do and most of them were unable to speak. Those who could speak appeared to understand Hungarian rather than Romanian.

Pat gently opened one of the doors to go in, but it was like trying to enter a cage of wild animals. The children rushed to the door and jumped on her, clawing and clinging, so that she had to unclasp their fingers and hands and back out. She found this a very hard thing to do, emotionally as well as physically. It was obvious that the children were desperate for help and love.

The two young Romanian girls who were in charge of each room in turn for one-and-a-half-hour periods had an impossible task: how could they occupy or amuse the children with no toys and no other facilities? None of the children had been trained to use a toilet. There was mess all over the rooms, in the corridors, on all the floors and over their clothes. Perhaps the most heart-rending sight of Pat's first visit to Remeti was the laundry, half filled by a huge pile of soiled bedlinen and dirty clothes. If that was what had accumulated after just three days, then after another three days there would most likely be no clean bedlinen and no clean clothes left. The children would have to go naked. The one poor girl struggling to remove the mess and clean everything could not cope. There were no washing machines and no tumbledryers.

It seemed clear that the most important way in which Pat could help this hospital would be to provide electricity, plumbing, washing machines and tumbledryers. The neglected state of the children newly arrived from Cadea was due to a lack of these 'luxuries' there also. At Cadea the children had been left naked and in their beds because there was only one cold tap in the whole building. However much goodwill was offered by the harassed staff in their new home, without proper washing facilities such neglect would be the continuing fate of the children at Remeti.

Pat and Margaret had heard a lot about Cadea during the drive from Cluj. It was a place for neuro-psychiatric and retarded children who were sent there at the end of their third year. It seemed to have served as a waiting room for death. Sixty or seventy children died every winter, their places being taken by the same number of new 'patients'. They became used to seeing their friends, or the boy or girl in the next bed, die.

One eleven-year-old boy called Viorel, whom they met at Remeti, had had an important job at Cadea, since he was such a helpful lad. He used to get up early in the morning and walk around to see which children had died. He would then carry out the little corpses and put them in what was called the mortuary. It was in fact just a large storeroom containing a table. In the winter when it was too cold for the wagons to come and take away the bodies, there was not enough room for them all on the table so he had to place them on the floor. He had felt rather panicky at times, he said, because he imagined that the eyes of the dead children were following him as he went out of the room. He had done this job for two years, before being moved to Remeti.

Pat had already heard nightmare stories about Cadea, but it was only when she met the children at Remeti that she could really believe them. She saw evidence there that the children had really been tied to their cots – apparently because there were only three women to look after more than one hundred and sixty children and otherwise they could not have coped. The majority had indeed been fastened to their cots, with cloths around their wrists and ankles; and if any became fractious their arms would be tied behind their backs too, so that they could not lash out. At Remeti the children were free, but the scarring on their bodies where they had struggled and chafed against the cloths which imprisoned them remained, as it probably would for the rest of their lives, as evidence of their suffering.

Pat had also heard stories of children rocking backwards and forwards and regurgitating. She saw not merely evidence but demonstrations of these habits at Remeti, where it happened quite frequently. Also, although the children were more free here, many were sitting up in their cots still unable to walk or even stand because they had never learnt how to do so. Many were scratching their faces and making animal noises. Pat had never seen such things before and neither, she discovered, had the Romanian girls at Remeti who were looking after the children.

They heard worse horror stories of Cadea. The three women in charge there had had to go home to their own families at seven o'clock at night, so they would lock up the whole place and put a bolt across the doors, having left some of the older children in charge. It was a great building in total darkness, as there were no electric light bulbs. Some of the older boys would prowl around making sure that the younger ones were behaving themselves and would arm themselves with lumps of wood or sticks, to keep control. One little boy, Josif, who had cried in his cot at the age of four, had been beaten round the head so brutally by one of the older boys that one eye imploded, and the lens of the other eye dropped out. When Pat and Margaret first met him at Remeti all he could see was a sort of fuzzy distinction between light and darkness.

They met another victim of even more appalling conditions. Some of the children at Cadea had been placed in the basement, in cellar-like storerooms off a long corridor. As they could not talk or sit up they were, from the age of three or four, simply wrapped up and laid down in cots. In one of the rooms there were five cots; the room had no windows, an earth floor and walls which were dripping wet. One boy, Dinu, had lived there for eight years. Other children had come and died or come and been moved upstairs, but Dinu had remained down there from the age of four and he had not seen light in all that time. When the children were 'rescued', or at least removed from Cadea, they were all naked and were given blankets. Dinu, used to the darkness, was terrified by the light and pulled his blanket over his head and stayed underneath it. When Pat first met him she half mistook his reluctance to come out of it as a game. Was he pretending the blanket was a tent? But when she lifted it a little to peep at him he firmly pulled it down. He was only tiny, but he was twelve years old and had enough strength to hold the blanket tightly down. He could neither walk nor talk; the only sounds he could make were those of the rats with whom he had shared the cellar.

The children in general seemed to resemble animals more than little human beings. They did not seem to understand much of what was being said to them, although this was partly because they had been used to Hungarian and not Romanian. Some could not speak at all, and even those who could were bewildered and confused by the change in their circumstances.

The Romanian girls from the village were doing their best to look after them, but seemed in some ways as bemused as their charges. When they had been offered the job they had been delighted at the idea of caring for poor and sick children: it would be wonderful, a good thing to do! But they were becoming rapidly disillusioned. Nothing had prepared them for the reality of the situation. They had no idea how to cope with these children who were not children, who did not know how to play or how to speak, and who, in spite of being eight, nine or ten years old, might not know how to walk. The girls were all quite horrified and panic-stricken at their helplessness, and at the fact that they would be held responsible if anything happened to a child in their care. They had twelve-hour shifts, and to be in the company of such creatures – who might tear their hair, scream, wet themselves, or worse – for so long was nerve-racking. On top of this, of course, was the increasing filth and lack of cleaning facilities. They were near to breakdown.

On the face of it, the situation was overwhelmingly hopeless. Remeti was only one among many such places, all in a similar state, all housing these traumatized creatures who had so far had no chance of life or even growth. How had any regime, any government in modern times, been allowed to cause such suffering, to destroy the lives of so many innocents?

2

The darkness

Nicolae Ceaucescu has been blamed since 1989 for the evil and suffering which oppressed the beautiful land of Romania, but not many years before that all had seemed so positive, and as the country's great leader, Ceaucescu had been given the title 'Source of our Light', receiving praise and honours from all over the world.

How had an ordinary peasant boy who had left school and home at the age of eleven to apprentice himself to a shoemaker in Bucharest turned first into a world leader and then into a monster? What sinister fairy tale is here?

Nicolae was born in 1918, one of ten children who lived with their parents – their mother a devout Christian and their father an atheist and an alcoholic – in a two-roomed cottage in the village of Scornicesti in Olt County. He was intelligent and hardworking, and has been described as charming but in no way exceptional. He had joined the Communist Party when he was fifteen and during his youth was frequently involved in anti-Fascist activities, being imprisoned two or three times. In 1945 he became Secretary of the Bucharest branch of the Party. After holding various other posts he was appointed Secretary General of the Romanian Communist Party in 1965 (on the death of Gheorghiu-Dej, whom he had met in prison and whose protégé he had been since the 1940s); President of the State Council (the top position in both party and state) in 1967; and President of Romania (a new post) in 1974. He was re-elected in 1980 and again in 1985.

Thus his position, and with it that of his country, must have seemed secure. But in 1989 he was overthrown and shot. Why? The most immediate reason was that he had stubbornly refused to be influenced by the wave of democratic liberation which was sweeping over Eastern European states, and had attempted to resist protests and dissent in his own country with increasingly mad brutality. He had inherited instability in a country suffering from a history of uncertain alliances, violence and cavalier decisions by outsiders (see Appendix B, pages 208–213). The instability within in his own character was to a large extent a product of this and in its turn caused further disaster and tragedy.

That Ceaucescu should, as a youth, have chosen Communism rather than Nazism, since these seemed the only real alternatives on offer, is understandable, as John Sweeney writes in his book *The Life and Evil Times of Nicolae Ceaucescu*:

For people who witnessed 1989, Marxism seems self-evidently bankrupt, but in the early '30s with the Great Depression battering capitalism and millions of people starving in the US and much of Europe and Romania too, its appeal was shining ... a Romanian teenager of peasant stock could be forgiven for believing it was better than what seemed the only alternative – Nazism. (page 36)

That he wanted to give his country and its people a sense of national identity and independence which had been missing during most of their history is commendable. His original intentions were no doubt sincere, and in his first years as leader he achieved much. But his ways of achieving his aims were often unwise or ruthless and his personality proved too vulnerable to the dangers associated with the wielding of power.

The nationalism Ceaucescu stressed was fed by xenophobia. There was antagonism towards the non-Romanian minorities. From the late 1960s discriminatory measures were taken against Hungarians and Germans, and in the '70s anti-Semitism was strengthened. He used the slogan 'Romanians must be masters in their own home' to justify policies which were disadvantageous to the 'cohabiting nationalities'.

In foreign policy his xenophobia was directed mainly against the Soviet Union. Although he was a convinced Communist he helped Romania, for various reasons, to edge away from and resist Soviet dominance, a process already begun in the days of his predecessor Gheorgiu-Dej, who in 1958 had secured Russia's agreement to the removal of its troops from Romanian soil. Coping with Russia continued to be the most important foreign policy question during Ceaucescu's time; and it was easier when Kruschev rather than Stalin was in power.

What Ceaucescu and the CPR (Communist Party of Romania) opposed most was the USSR's strategic economic plan under its version of the Common Market – COMECON – for its satellite countries in Europe. This envisaged industrial growth for East Germany and Czechoslovakia, while Romania was to close its heavy industrial factories and function merely as a breadbasket.

Russia had always been a traditional enemy of Romania and in spite of his communism Ceaucescu continued to distance his country from the Soviet Union. He refused to be drawn into Moscow's anti-Chinese and anti-Yugoslav campaigns. He defended the Spanish and Italian Euro-Communists against criticism; he gave sanctuary in Romania to the anti-Soviet wing of the Greek Communist party; he even expelled members of the pro-Moscow faction from the country. He condemned the Soviet occupation of Afghanistan and apparently defied Moscow by sending athletes to the 1984 Olympic Games in Los Angeles.

In May 1966, on the eve of a visit to Bucharest by the new Soviet leader Leonid Brezhnev, he denounced 'military blocs and the existence of military bases and troops in foreign countries as an anachronism incompatible with the independence and national sovereignty of the peoples, and normal relations between states'. In 1968 he denounced the invasion of Czechoslovakia by the Warsaw Pact troops; he saw it as 'a great mistake and a grave danger to peace in Europe, to the fate of socialism in the world ... a shameful moment in the history of the revolutionary movement ... there is no justification whatsoever for military intervention in the affairs of a fraternal socialist state ... the entire Romanian people will not allow anyone to violate the territory of our homeland ... we shall never betray our homeland ... we shall never betray the interests of our people'.

This speech made him a national hero overnight. There were rumours that Russia would invade. He might become a martyr. His stature increased in the West as well as at home. David Binder of the *New York Times* wrote in 1966, 'It may now be appropriate to say that Nicolae Ceaucescu is the man who has taken charge of the breaking up of the Soviet Empire.' Congratulations and adulation increased. Here was an East European leader who could stand up to Russia and survive.

His anti-Soviet stance brought immediate dividends and awards – membership of the General

Agreement on Tariffs and Trade; membership of the IMF and the World Bank. In 1975 Romania was granted the status of 'Most Favoured Nation' by the US Government. During the next decade it received a billion dollars of US backed credits as well as access to advanced computer technology, light machine guns and military helicopters.

The West wooed him in other ways. Pilgrimages began. In the late 1960s and '70s he hosted visits from world leaders: De Gaulle, President Nixon, Margaret Thatcher, Harold Wilson, President Jimmy Carter, Julian Amery, Edward Heath, David Steel, Brezhnev, Honeker, Husack, President Agostinho Neto of Angola, President Mathieu Kerkou of Benin, Prime Minister Todor Zhivkov of Bulgaria, and Edward Gierek of Poland.

As well as hosting eminencies at home he was whirling round the world visiting others abroad. After 1975 he visited Tito of Yugoslavia, President Felix Houphouet-Boingny of the Ivory Coast, Prime Minister Todor Zhivkov of Bulgaria, Janos Kodai of Hungary, President Ernesto Geisel of Brazil, President Alfonso Lopez of Colombia and Jose Figueres Ferrer of Costa Rica.

1978 marked the height of Ceaucescu's acceptability in the West. In April he and his wife paid an official visit to Washington. Then he called on President Giscard d'Estang in France. In mid-June they stayed at Buckingham Palace for three days, and between

January and October 1978 he paid state visits to no less than thirteen countries: Ghana, Liberia, Guinea, Mauritania, Pakistan, Indonesia, Australia and Vietnam, Mongolia, Kenya, Egypt, China and North Korea. In 1979 he went to Iran and laid a wreath at the tomb of Ayatollah Khomeini.

Honours were bestowed on him. At Buckingham Palace the Queen made him a Knight Grand Cross of the Order of the Bath. The Danes gave him the Order of the Elephant. Austria, Italy and West Germany gave medals and awards. Giscard d'Estang awarded him the Insignia of a Commander of the Legion d'Honneur. Amidst his medals and awards was a certificate of honorary citizenship of Disneyland. In a letter of January 1983 Nixon referred to Ceaucescu as 'one of the greatest leaders of the world who valiantly carries out an independent foreign policy'. Harold Wilson wrote, 'The more visitors he gets and the more visits he makes the more countries (he hopes) will protect him against any Russian intervention.'

No one in Romania was allowed to forget the honours and flatteries which Western governments poured onto the maverick ruler. The National History Museum in Bucharest had a floor devoted to 'homage' to Ceaucescu and his wife. The salons were filled with honours, medals, awards and degrees from all corners of the world, set out in cabinets according to the continent of origin.

Bishop Mervyn Stockwood wrote an article called 'The Big Improvements', welcoming Ceaucescu's state visit to Britain in 1978, which was published in *The Times*: 'Each year I have noticed a higher standard of living,' the Bishop wrote in his eulogy of 'the brave man' whose 'exceedingly generous treatment of the churches in Romania was something of which we in Britain might well be envious.'

The adulation he received from world leaders elevated him in the eyes of many Romanians but aroused bitterness in others who were experiencing hardship and oppression.

The Securitate were not only good at orchestrating popular shows of adoration of the leader; it was an elite security force which held allegiance only to him and could be brutal in suppressing dissent. The Securitate was in the hands of one of Nicolae's brothers – indeed thirty members of his close family were said to have prominent positions in the country; this nepotism was protection to him and also helped him to amass a personal fortune.

His luxurious lifestyle alongside the fact that many of his economic policies failed, occasioned further unrest. In the '80s he determined to pay off Romania's external debt of more than $10 billion and exported most agricultural and manufactured goods, thus creating domestic shortages of food, fuel, energy and other necessities.

In spite of its enormous potential, agriculture was underfunded and foodstuffs had to be imported. Yet a trade surplus was maintained by restricting imports and exporting most of the country's industrial as well as agricultural produce. Goods were scarce yet expensive and the prices of some household goods tripled. Meat was almost unobtainable and bread was rationed, as was petrol, which hardly mattered to the owners of private cars as their use was prohibited during the winter months. The use of vacuums and refrigerators was also banned. There was no street lighting in rural areas, and it was impossible to obtain pharmaceutical products and antibiotics. These were as rare as coffee, rice and sugar.

Power was rationed. The daily supply allowed in winter was equivalent to one hour's warmth from one bar of an electric fire. The gas pressure was not strong enough for cooking. Ceaucescu blamed the high interest rates of foreign bankers for plundering Romania's economy. As the population became more wretched he compensated for this by creating a facade of success and splendour in which he wallowed. The streets, empty of cars, accented the splendour of his Mercedes as it rolled along. Television and newspaper coverage concentrated on his great popularity and success. He spent billions on grandiose building projects. And perhaps most dangerous of all were his plans for systemization, whereby the agriculture of Romania was to be revolutionized and in the process undermined.

He planned – and had indeed started – to destroy hundreds of villages, in favour of new industrial complexes.

All dissent was ruthlessly suppressed. Opponents of the regime disappeared and might have been discovered in the Dr Petra Groza Hospital being treated for 'political paranoia'. Anyone who suggested that there were civil rights abuses might be rushed into intensive care suffering from 'senile dementia'. Journalists were in particular danger since they were not only in possession of the real news about what was going on but were in the perilous position of having to inform the wider world. So they were likely to be diagnosed as having a variety of mental ailments – persecution complexes, 'discordant character structure' and so on – and locked away with genuinely insane patients; and like them they might be forced to make their own coffins in preparation for a death by unknown means. The abuse of psychiatry to subdue dissent has been well documented in the Soviet Union. It was also widely used in Romania as reports by Amnesty International, which kept track of it, prove. If these reports were read by those who danced attendance on Ceaucescu, they gave no sign.

The Great Typewriter Decree of 1983 was presumably intended to prevent news of what was really happening in Romania from being spread abroad. It ruled that the renting or lending of typewriters was forbidden; to own a typewriter one had to have permission from the police. Anyone wanting to purchase one had to give samples of their typing to the police with an explanation of why they wanted one. If a typewriter had to be repaired it needed a new certificate, as did its owner. There were other legal steps to be taken when inheriting or disposing of such a lethal machine.

This decree seems to prove two things – the poor state of a regime which believed it had to be (or could be) protected in this way and, more worryingly, the poor state of mind of the Dictator. For that is what Ceaucescu was becoming.

It seems to be generally agreed that it was Ceaucescu's trip to North Korea in 1971 which excited him with the ambition of becoming a dictator in the model of Kim Il Sung. Certainly at some time paranoia and extreme egotism leading to megalomania must have set in. Some of his actions were bizarre in the extreme.

If there was any logic at all in his behaviour it was that he wanted to make Romania great and so he had to be great too. In 1978 a new underground station was being built in Bucharest and an enormous hole had been excavated for the construction of the entrance. One morning the engineer in charge of the project returned to find his hole had disappeared. In its place there was a piece of parkland complete with trees and benches, which had apparently 'materialized' overnight. Ceaucescu had been distraught to find a huge hole in the exact spot where he had been planning to make a welcoming speech to new students of Bucharest Polytechnic and had ordered its removal. Hundreds of workmen, troops, gardeners and landscapers had worked through the night to repair the park. Turf was taken from other parks and trees were uprooted from other parts of the city. All was finished by 6 a.m., when the engineer returned, not to work but to stare in disbelief.

Another time it was a huge building rather than a hole which had to disappear. Ceaucescu had planned a Boulevard of Socialist Victory in Bucharest and ordered the demolition of all the properties of the Old City which obstructed the route. The old houses were simply demolished. Many old people lived in them and they were simply thrown out onto the pavements; some of them were forced to sign papers requesting the destruction of their houses and were even sent bills for the job. Some committed suicide. One building remained intact but obtrusive – the Brancenvose Hospital. Its basement was infected by rats and the staff had introduced cats to deal with the problem. On one of Ceaucescu's visits to the hospital his dog Colonel Corbu chased and fought one of the cats; both antagonists were hurt, and Ceaucescu drove away, furious. His beloved Corbu had been assaulted and his nose bloodied. The fury gave rise to a new edict. The Brancenvose Hospital must come down.

Within days it was in ruins; the year before it had treated about 50,000 Romanians.

Colonel Corbu was a beautiful black Labrador which David Steel had sent as a puppy to Ceaucescu as a 'thank you' for hospitality. The people at first had referred to the dog as 'Comrade Corbu', since it accompanied Ceaucescu everywhere. It was to be seen travelling behind him in its own limousine. Ceaucescu soon provided it with a bitch, Sherone, to keep it company. During the day the dogs slept in their own flat, which was complete with luxury furnishing, television and telephone. At night Corbu slept with Ceaucescu. The Securitate made sure that no one other than a specially appointed doctor would give food to the dogs – after tasting it himself. Ceaucescu's paranoia, a common trait of dictators, extended to his dogs. The Romanian ambassador in London was under orders to buy British dog biscuits and Winalot which were then sent to Bucharest in the diplomatic bag. According to one source the dogs were served steak in golden bowls. He loved his dogs; his children were thrown to the wolves.

This was, ironically, a side effect of his desire for a great Romania, a population great in numbers, and great in the 'purity' and perfection of its people. But it all went horribly wrong and ended as the most disastrous and cruel tragedy of his regime.

To increase his man- and woman-power he did not just appeal to families to 'provide' more children if they responsibly could, but he ordered them directly to do so. He did what he could to enforce this policy of 'fast breeding'. Couples were encouraged to have five, six, or even seven children; a large family was 'a sign of loyalty to the regime'; a house with many children was 'proof of a good citizen's concern for the nation's future'; a pregnant woman was 'everyone's concern'. Population growth must no longer, in Romania, be regarded as a spontaneous phenomenon; it must be managed and controlled.

His wife Elena was his chief conspirator in the campaign. She was the ostensible representative of women's interests and as Chairperson of the National Women's Council she was in charge of the policies which were put into action to achieve the population explosion. Abortions were no longer allowed as a method of birth control, neither was contraception. Penalties for doctors who helped in illegal abortions were severe; all women between the ages of sixteen and forty-five had to undergo gynaecological checks to make sure that they were not using contraceptive devices. The Roman Catholic Church's ban on abortion and contraception is based on its particular understanding of theology and morality – i.e. the primary purpose of and justification of sex is procreation; Ceaucescu did not presume to take either a moral or a theological stand. He simply wanted more Romanians. Indeed, just as in Nazi Germany Himmler castigated old-fashioned moral and religious prejudices against illegitimacy, so Elena's journalists preached the same doctrine – that unmarried mothers were just as acceptable as married ones.

The policies worked. The number of babies born rose from 273,687 in 1966 to 527,784 in 1967. While births in 1967 went up by 92.8 per cent, however, infant mortality figures rose by 145.6 per cent. An anonymous writer in the *New York Times*, quoted by John Sweeney, wrote that it took nine months to double the number of new-born babies and six years to double the number of gynaecologists, obstetricians, paediatricians, midwives, houses, hospitals, orphanages, baby milk and clothes to care for them.

Ceaucescu had virtually 'fathered' thousands of children, but had taken no thought and no action to provide for them. The families themselves simply could not cope with the extra burden. Hundreds of babies, even those who were healthy, were abandoned, just left in some public place or taken to a hospital and not reclaimed; hundreds more were physically or mentally handicapped, a few had Aids, though the disease had not been officially recognized by the regime; many were entirely unwanted by anyone, some were despised because of their particular ethnic origin. Hundreds died.

Irresponsible parenthood, whether the parents be a couple or a political or religious regime, parenthood which, for whatever reasons, allows and encourages children to be born without first ensuring that they are adequately provided both with food and clothing and with a loving environment, must be one of the greatest crimes on earth. Was this crime really unknown to the outside world?

It was actually the destruction of thirty churches and monasteries in Bucharest to make way for a Civic Centre which first aroused Western criticism of Ceaucescu's rule on a grand scale. In the mid-1980s tourists and journalists returned from Bucharest with stories and photos of churches which had been demolished or even moved wholesale to sites which were more favourable to Ceaucescu's plans for redesigning his city. People in Western Europe were incensed by such sacrilege. The shocking state of his children had existed for many years by this time, of course, but perhaps the West really was ignorant of this particular outrage. Sick and immobile children are far easier to hide from prying eyes than a church building.

After the revolution in 1989, however, the orphanages were open to the public and the full horror of the situation began to emerge. John Sweeney describes his visit to one 'hospital' in *The Life and Evil Times of Nicolae Ceaucescu*:

They were left to rot in out-of-the way hospitals and clinics. The Romanians called them the 'irrecuperables'; literally unrecoverable. The official policy was that they were so sick no resources should be wasted on them. I only visited one such hospital for 'irrecuperables', Platarest, about twenty miles from Bucharest. It was enough.

Grey walls, white ceiling, cement floor, no toys. Far worse than their sick bodies – unnaturally white, with limbs like sticks, frail trunks topped by huge, domed heads – was the noise the children made. It was a click-click-click sound, dry, not loud, like something a big insect might make. It took a while before we realised they were grinding their teeth. They lay, some of them four to a cot dotted with flies like currants on dough. The nurses looking after them impressed me as doing the best they could, but they seemed utterly without the benefit of medical training, lacking proper drugs, medical equipment, drips, nappies and good food for the children. There were, in all, three nurses and two cleaners looking after one hundred and seven children. There were no doctors on duty that day.

One little click-click-click boy lay on his cot shaking his head and rolling to and fro, to and fro. His name was Emil Teodorescu, aged four. He was half the size of my son, not yet two. His mother, the nurse said, had tried to have an abortion but she didn't succeed. He was suffering from 'Hepatitis B'. The nurse looked around

the ward and said most of them came from
Bucharest. Before the revolution they had 1,9
Lei a day for each child for medicines, that's lit-
tle over a penny.

The next ward was better, with two children
to a cot. There were flies again feeding at one
child's mouth, and the teeth-grinding noise.
One child was foaming at the mouth, his oppo-
site number in the cot was staring dully at him.
Infections were a danger. The next ward was the
hepatitis isolation unit. One child had sores on
its leg; the stench of urine stung the nostrils.
Another child had sores on its head. The fourth
ward stank like a farmyard. It was full of older
children screaming, wafting flies away, rocking
to and fro, to and fro. Before the revolution, the
nurse said, they had no-one to complain to.

On the way out of the hospital a red-framed
notice board hung in a place of honour where,
before the revolution, they had pinned up a
photograph of Nicolae Ceaucescu, President of
Romania. (pages 141–2)

Scenes such as this were reported from all over
Romania. Thousands of children were in this plight.
Many were dying or half starved. Those who survived
might be tied to their cots, and Pat had seen the
resultant scars on the children's limbs at Remeti: the
extent of the mental scars was unimaginable and still

to be fully assessed. The children were fed twice a day out of buckets, or were given injections alternating with a meal so that they made less mess. They were all suffering from cold and neglect. Many were deformed and ill but untended by any medical care. Some, like Dinu at Cadea, had been kept in total darkness.

This situation had existed for years, apparently unknown to the outside world. 'Ceaucescu's children' they had been christened, for they were all the victims of his regime. Now their careless 'father' was gone, and the Herculean task of restoring them to life was a burden on others' shoulders.

3

A candle in the darkness

As Pat and Margaret left Remeti after that first, agonizing visit and headed back to Truro, they thought of the warehouse full of all the things the good folk of Cornwall had collected – soap, teddy bears, clothes. Now they knew the reality of the situation, would these goods be of any immediate use?

Once on the plane home they began to prioritize. The very first task must be to send out a team to work on the electrics and the plumbing at Remeti. Too few electric light bulbs coupled to a very rickety wiring system failed to light the hospital adequately. There were only two toilets working in the whole building; the rest were all solidly blocked. They would use some of the money which had been collected to buy washing machines, and they needed a reliable power supply in order to run these as well as support the lighting system. One constant image before their eyes was that of the Romanian girl in the laundry hopelessly trying to wash a huge pile of soiled clothes and sheets in a bath, with just one tap of cold water. Thank God for plumbers and electricians.

The first thing Pat did when she was back was to put out an announcement to everyone who had shown an interest in the project so far, and also through Radio Cornwall, that she urgently needed plumbers and electricians willing to go out to Romania. At once a team of men from the Satellite Earth Station at Goonhilly Downs volunteered, and E. Thomas, a builder in Falmouth, offered materials and manpower to take care of the plumbing.

With the promise of skilled manpower secure, Pat gathered together all those involved and reported exactly what she had found in Remeti. They decided that the first big convoy must take food and clothes, plus those priceless washing machines. The plan was for the electricians and plumbers to set off early in a mini-convoy of two vehicles, so that by the time the main convoy arrived with the washing machines they would have done their job of preparing the ground. They certainly fulfilled everyone's hopes: when the main convoy reached Remeti shortly after Easter 1991, the hospital was almost completely rewired and the necessary plumbing was in place.

It seems significant and even symbolic that those eminently practical men were required to be first on the scene, making preparations which were, and have always continued to be, absolutely essential to the programme which aimed to rescue and restore the children. Rudyard Kipling's poem 'The Sons of Martha' says it all:

> The Sons of Mary seldom bother, for they
>   have inherited that good part;
> But the Sons of Martha favour their
>   Mother of the careful soul and the
>   troubled heart.
> And because she lost her temper once,
>   and because she was rude to the Lord
>   her Guest,
> Her Sons must wait upon Mary's Sons,
>   world without end, reprieve or rest.
>
> It is their care in all the ages to take the
>   buffet and cushion the shock.
> It is their care that the gear engages; it is
>   their care that the switches lock.
> It is their care that the wheels run truly; it is
>   their care to embark and entrain,
> Tally, transport, and deliver duly the Sons
>   of Mary by land and main...
>
> They do not preach that their God will
>   rouse them a little before the nuts work
>   loose.
> They do not teach that His Pity allows
>   them to drop their job when they damn
>   well choose.

As in the thronged and the lighted ways, so
in the dark and the desert they stand,
Wary and watchful all their days that their
brethren's days may be long in the land.

Raise ye the stone or cleave the wood to make
some a path more fair or flat –
Lo, it is black already with blood some Son
of Martha spilled for that!
Not as a ladder from earth to Heaven, not
as a witness to any creed,
But simple service simply given to his own
kind in their common need.

And the Sons of Mary smile and are blessed
– they know the Angels are on their side.
They know in them is the Grace confessed,
and for them are the Mercies multiplied.
They sit at the Feet – they hear the Word –
they see how truly the Promise runs.
They have cast their burden upon the Lord,
and – the Lord He lays it on Martha's
Sons!

Just after the plumbers and electricians had completed the work at Remeti, and before Pat had set off with
the first convoy, the German Red Cross had contacted
her.

'We hear you've got plumbers in Romania.'

'Yes.'

'Would you mind asking them to go up to the baby hospital at Satu Mare?'

'Certainly.'

So Pat contacted the men, glad that after all some coordination was possible with the German Red Cross, and told them exactly how to get to the baby hospital. They went up to Satu Mare, quite keen to help in whatever way was necessary. They were shocked to find that many of the six hundred and fifty babies there were without clothes as the washing facilities were so poor. But they did not know whether to laugh or cry when they saw the particular problem they were being asked to solve. The German Red Cross had delivered to the hospital a huge commercial washing machine that was too big to go through the door to the kitchen. It was standing outside, still wearing its steel bands and cardboard cladding. Workmen were trying to dismantle the door and stone door posts in order to get the machine inside. But Pat's plumbers, those eminently practical men, told them not to bother. The hospital would not have the power to operate it, and this machine had a two-hour cycle which was quite useless while the water supply was limited to one hour in the morning and one in the afternoon.

For all their practicality and skill they were powerless to help until the local power and water systems had been improved. They looked on, horrified, as the women struggled to wash all the clothes by hand. All they could do was to leave their electrical and plumbing equipment behind, ready for when it might be of some use.

They returned to Cornwall just before the first big White Cross Mission convoy left on Easter Day, 1991. This, with eight vehicles, is still the biggest convoy ever to have left, but it established a firm tradition that Easter Sunday is the day when a convoy, of whatever size, sets off from Truro to Romania. Everyone who participates goes to his or her church first and the convoy sets off in the afternoon. Something new at Easter! It seems appropriate to White Cross supporters that the emphasis of the day is on setting off to do something of immense practical service.

That first convoy delivered loads of food and clothes in addition to the desperately needed washing machines, and those who travelled with the vans did all they could during their two-week stay to make the place as comfortable as possible, working flat out for the whole of their visit.

One worry – and an important one – was that the Romanian girls who were looking after the children were becoming increasingly distressed and out of their depth. When they had first gone to care for the children arriving from Cadea, they had been, in spite of the difficulties and the daily crises, enthusiastic to do what they could. But now only two months later they were on the point of giving up and were not even attempting to clean the place. In spite of the plumbing which had been done, some of the toilets were not working properly, there was broken glass and mess all over the place and the children were out of control. It was obvious that Dr Oprea was going to lose staff. The only thing keeping them there was apparently the meagre salary of £20 a month; it was probably the first salary they had ever received and they might never get another one. How long would they last out even for this? That Easter there was a real sense of despair.

It was clear to Pat and her team of supporters that not only electrics, plumbing, food and clothes were needed, but also an additional supply of helpers, who would work alongside the Romanian staff, encouraging and assisting them as well as the children. These extra helpers would have to be volunteers, as the White Cross Mission had not yet found its millionaire!

So began the 'reign of the childcare volunteers'. Four volunteers had gone out with the first Easter convoy in 1991. Since then more than five hundred people, mainly young, mainly from Cornwall, have travelled to Romania. Without their unique and individual contributions, the lives of the children in their care would have been immeasurably poorer.

From the beginning the administration and organization of the childcare volunteer scheme was the responsibility of Jeff Saville, Deputy Section Head of the Continuing Education Division of Cornwall County Council. He and his wife left Cornwall in 1994 and Sue Pearce, the White Cross Mission's secretary, took over the task from then on.

Most volunteers work for periods of between one and twelve months, doing what they can, singly or in groups, to help the Romanian staff in caring for the children. The qualifications are minimal but vital. They must be at least eighteen years old, in good health, and love children. Many preface their applications with the words: 'I don't have any skills but I do like children.'

To like, or better to love children has certainly proved to be the prime quality needed. At first it was expected that most applicants would be those who had some specialist or professional interest in or expertise with children. Hardly any such people applied, but those who did – nurses, teachers, doctors and social workers – have been excellent and greatly appreciated. Equally appreciated, however, are the contributions of the 'average' untrained people with an instinctive love of children and a warmth of personality which allows that love its natural expression. A considerable measure of unselfishness and a mature self-discipline are also essential, and a sunny nature is a great asset!

Volunteers have to pay their own fare and expenses and be able to live harmoniously with people they do not know very well, in crowded conditions.

Above all they have to be prepared to expect – and deal with – the unexpected. New volunteers are asked to attend an initial information evening and if they are still interested they are asked to explain more about themselves, their likes, dislikes, talents and attitude to life. They do not have to be Christians, for while the White Cross has a Christian heart, it is not an evangelical mission. They are fully briefed on what living in Romania will be like, where they will live, and, as well as being told to expect the unexpected, they are prepared for what will be expected of them in turn.

Jeff Saville and Sue Pearce have done their best to ensure that all volunteers genuinely care for children and are mainly motivated by compassion and a strong desire, even a longing, to help. However, the volunteers are not candidates for canonization but human beings, most of them young and in the process of finding themselves (not necessarily just a prerogative for young people!). There are likely to be other motives in addition to compassion for the children: one might just have broken up with a boyfriend or girlfriend, another might want to escape temporarily from a troubling family situation. Others may be unhappy about the direction their life is taking, or even feel uneasy that they are in too comfortable a rut. Doing something entirely different might shock them into an awareness of who and what they are – and what the world is like for others. Pat is a great believer in encouraging young people to get out and involved in situations beyond anything they have experienced before. Facing and coping with a new challenge invariably increases self-confidence and self-belief, and can open up all sorts of possibilities for later life which might otherwise have been entirely missed.

In Victorian times well-educated (and wealthy) young men would embark on a 'grand tour', travelling abroad and experiencing the culture of other countries. Today it is common for young people of both sexes and all classes to seek some pre- or postgraduate experience by taking a year off and travelling or working abroad. This quite natural and indeed excellent impulse to pack one's books away and take up a rucksack is no doubt there in the motivation of many of the White Cross volunteers. Pat herself remembers how, after she had qualified as a teacher of Religious Education in 1960 and had been teaching at Chartham Secondary School for four years, she returned home one evening and placed a pile of books she had to mark on the table. Feeling tired, she sat down, suddenly swept away the books with one hand and reached for the *Times Educational Supplement* with the other. She applied for six jobs at various places abroad and was offered all of them. It was an act which no doubt expressed frustration at a possibly humdrum existence and a desire for a more adventurous life. It took her to Tanzania where, after teaching for a year, she met and married Denis Owen Robson. They lived in Nairobi, where she gave birth to her son Philip in 1966.

The White Cross Mission volunteers have varying expectations. Some have become increasingly apprehensive or nervous as they have neared the Romanian border or Remeti itself. Others who were perhaps over confident when they went out have been shaken to find that at first they could hardly cope. A rare few over the years have decided, or been gently persuaded, that it would be wise for them to return to England. Many have become addicted and have returned to Romania once, twice or even three times to help further. For almost all the volunteers it has been a maturing experience from which they have learned a great deal. It has introduced many to their life's vocation, and a few have had their lives changed dramatically.

All the volunteers admit they find before long that they have favourites among the children. They all go out intending not to, but they all end up spending a bit more time with one child rather than another. It is inevitable in 'normal' life to relate more easily, happily and fruitfully with some people rather than others. At Remeti this was discouraged at first, because it might seem to suggest to some children who were not so popular that they had been marked out for isolation or rejection, but it was found that it actually did more good than harm. Pat, in a poignant comment on this subject, said, 'If a special bond exists between a volunteer and child for only one month it means that once in its life that child is special to someone. And *even if it might not be special to anyone ever again* that one month's special friendship might be the trigger that starts a child on the road to recovery.'

One question which concerned those responsible for the programme and the volunteers themselves was whether the constant coming and going of different personalities would unsettle the children, and might be harmful for their long-term relationships. In fact the children appear to take this in their stride. 'Who's coming next?' they ask. 'When's so and so coming?' It has not seemed to worry them at all. They have the Romanian staff, the doctor and the manager or coordinator of the programme always with them, so they do have some stability.

It has also seemed to some volunteers that because they go out for such short periods, it must mean that they have not done anything of significance. In fact every volunteer makes a great contribution towards the success of the whole venture, as Ella Delderfield shows in the following account called 'Rodika I love you', just one experience among many at Remeti's sister hospital Bratca.

I didn't have a favourite child when I went to Romania – each and every one of them had their own brand of peculiar charm which I grew to adore. But some children stuck out in my mind more than others, probably the ones I found the hardest to deal with.

The first time I saw Rodika all she was was a bundle of urine-soaked grey blankets. Lifting the covers cautiously I was scared of this creature who opened her mouth to scream at me, simultaneously pinching her face till it bled. In fact she was so self abusive that I had been at Bratca a month before I found the courage to coax her out of her cot. Rodika did nothing but bang her head against the floor and bawl. Hannah and I wrestled with her to try and lift her back into her safe little world under her blanket.

Which is when I caught her off guard and, in a moment of impulsive bravery, stroked her face gently with my fingers. To my amazement she didn't bite them, instead she gazed up at me with big brown frightened eyes. I was smitten. We took her outside and sat her down with each of us holding one hand to stop her pinching herself. Hannah rubbed her back slowly while I sang to her taking care to look into her eyes and not at the red scars stretching down her face which she had made with her fingernails.

This girl is twelve years old, I thought, she does not speak and is so full of anger or fear that she hurts herself all day long. Were we getting through to her?

When she blew us a kiss, we grinned in relief and happiness. Rodika was reaching out to us, from somewhere in that muddled mind she was responding to us holding her gently. Perhaps no-one had shown her any compassion before.

Every morning for nearly three weeks, either I or Hannah would sit quietly on a chair with that little girl. Such a small thing to do; and yet it made such a difference! Progress was slow, and rewards were few for our time and patience. One day she smiled and laughed when we tickled her unintentionally, and soon she recognized us when we walked into her salon.

It is now a week before I leave Romania. Rodika has changed so much but she still has a long way to go. She smiles and laughs when she is picked up and no longer abuses herself continuously. The scars on her face are healing over and I dare to hope that the trauma clouding her mind is starting to clear a little.

At the end of her account Ella quotes Mother Teresa: 'We can do not great things, only small things with great love.'

4

Great love

Great love was surely needed by the first childcare volunteers; they (and the maintenance men) were the real pioneers and heroes. The children they faced were unlike any they had ever seen, and the conditions in the hospital were appalling. Some of the toilets were still not in working order, even after the initial efforts of the plumbers, and there were no baths or showers. Hot water in Remeti was available only for two hours on a Thursday and two on a Sunday. There was a mad rush to wash as many filthy children as possible during these times. Every window was smashed as soon as it was replaced. There was excrement all over the corridors and in the salons. The summer flies were unbearable. Forty-five of the sixty children could not walk and many more did not speak. They were good, however, at making weird noises, by day and night. It was discovered quite soon that the doctor in charge (Dr Oprea) was an alcoholic and a megalomaniac.

Early in the summer of 1991, two caravans were towed across Europe and placed under the doctor's flat in the orphanage yard as a home for six volunteers. They were never free of the children and their nights were disturbed by the doctor's dogs, which slept under the caravans during the day and howled at the wolves in the hills by night. As winter set in it began to get very cold in the caravans at night. A deal was done with the manager of a construction company who lived in the village, to allow the volunteers to live in a flat which soon became known as the 'English House'. It was made of wood and was alive with fleas. The toilets did not work, the sink kept parting from the wall and hot water was available – on a rota – for four hours a week. However, the volunteers were not left to struggle alone with their difficulties.

Fate had arranged for another special, and quite unexpected, volunteer to be waiting for them in Remeti ready to help. Jahal de Meritens was a volunteer who had originally been supported by a small French organization which had run out of money and was unable to maintain a full programme. Born in Madagascar, he had a benign and charismatic personality. He had arrived in Remeti in February 1991 and Pat invited him to be part of the White Cross Mission. He was a child psychologist who had already worked with children in care and he wanted to give himself wholeheartedly to the Romanian 'irrecuperables', spurred on to urgent action by the fear (groundless, as it turned out) that he had a brain tumour and did not have long to live.

It was Jahal who spearheaded the first childcare programme, but he created it together with the first English volunteers. They all found that, whatever theories and preconceptions they had come with, these all faded as soon as they faced the children. It was they who dictated what must be done to meet their needs and the volunteers simply had to learn what was right as they went along. In Jahal's words:

> When we arrived in Romania ... some of the volunteers had a sound knowledge and much experience in working with disabled children and we were ready to apply that knowledge to the Romanian orphans. Then, we saw the children – and all our knowledge and experience counted for nothing. We knew that we didn't know. We knew that we had to learn but nobody could teach us except the children themselves. Therefore we forgot our experience, our theories, and we started to watch and to listen carefully. Later we put together our thoughts and tried unsuccessfully to build a therapy. At least we discovered that the children needed love and attention.

One of the first English volunteers was Graham Banks. Graham had flown out to Remeti at the same time as the Easter '91 convoy. Graham was a Day Services Manager with the Social Services in Cornwall and had already been out to Romania in 1990, working with another group for a few months, but he transferred his commitment to the White Cross Mission because he felt it to be more spiritually inspired. He and two colleagues went out to Remeti with the specific intention of 'assessing' the children, discovering or confirming their age, sex and names. Some of the children did not even have names so had to be 'christened' on the spot. Some had three versions of their name – Hungarian, Romanian and Gypsy. They compared their lists with those of Dr Oprea to establish a definitive record of the children in care at Remeti.

Meeting Jahal was a memorable experience for Graham. He himself had worked for years caring for children and adults with learning difficulties. They talked throughout the night, drinking *palinka* (plum brandy) and trying to puzzle out how they could best help these children. They had all suffered traumas of a nightmarish quality; but they were nightmares which did not vanish with the dawn as dreams do. They lingered, parts of them visible still. No one would ever know exactly what hells these children had experienced and only the future, they felt, would reveal how deep-rooted the damage was.

The children had also been severely deprived of all normal nourishment – food, warmth, a stimulating environment, the presence and company of others, and above all human warmth and love, vital for spontaneous growth. Their development into mature adulthood had been delayed, perhaps permanently. Because of its utter vulnerability a baby needs to be, and usually is, the focus of complete care. It cannot be neglected for a moment. A small child is similarly entirely dependent on the sensitivity and care of others. The parents are endowed with instinctive awareness of its needs and know that it must also gradually develop its own being. These children had had little or none of such nurture and stimulation; what they had been deprived of could be summed up in two words: 'love' and 'attention'. The volunteers had to be willing to touch, hold and cuddle, to befriend each child in whatever way was possible, to play or do things together, to encourage and praise, to stimulate and to respond to whatever challenge the child offered, to try to understand aggression or strange behaviour and sometimes to discipline with gentleness.

After a short stay Graham had to return to his full-time job in England, but Jahal, with the help of the other volunteers, worked on. First he separated the extremely disturbed children from the others and settled them in a day room known simply as 'Salon 6'. At the same time he set apart special rooms in the basement, each designed to introduce the children to some of the normal pleasures and activities of childhood. One has equipment for simple gymnastics, another is essentially a play room and has plenty of toys. There is an art room where the children can experiment with colour and paint and learn how to create pictures and images; and a relaxation or 'sensory' room, painted a soothing shade of blue, where aromatherapy – with music and a special oil for each individual child – can be administered. The music room contains instruments which the volunteers can play and which the children might be able to try.

A volunteer will usually, or ideally, take just one child at a time into one of these special rooms and if he or she is unable to paint or play, the time will be spent just sitting on the volunteer's lap. Through this individual attention and close contact the child should begin to gain confidence in itself, in adults and in life. The volunteer is trained to notice every little response, any suggestion of unease, any little sign of happiness and normality as the child's personality begins to unfold while it experiments with a toy or musical instrument or starts to hum or sing. As Jahal wrote, 'These children must learn to play.' When they play they start to relate to each other; they have to obey a few basic rules, they can safely express their fantasies, fears and tensions. Their energy can function in a positive way and moreover they can have fun.

These children had been innocents in prison when they should have been running around in the fresh air, surrounded by sunlight and all the exhilarating sights and sounds of the beautiful country into which they had been born, and all the excitement of a universe of which they were as yet entirely unaware. Carefree *joie de vivre* is the birthright of every child – but so many of these children could hardly even walk at an age when most children would already have started school.

For those who could walk, however, one enduringly favourite activity started by Jahal was the daily disco, half an hour before dinner. The children delight in it, and of course it is very healthy physically and psychologically, as are the walks around the spital in the lovely Romanian countryside, which the volunteers enjoy as much as the children.

Jahal painstakingly established his programme of care and apart from one problem everything was going well. The White Cross Mission was paying him a small salary. He was cleared of the fear that he had a brain tumour. He had met and fallen in love with Karen, one of the English volunteers. The White Cross Mission had been asked to take care of another twenty-four children at an orphanage in Bratca, five miles from Remeti. And the Director of Health had acquired a more hospitable dwelling for the volunteers – the 'Woodhouse'.

The one problem was that Dr Oprea, who was in charge of the hospital, was an alcoholic. He had been one for some time, but when his hospital was suddenly overcrowded by the children from Cadea, his addiction increased. The responsibility for so many children in such appalling conditions was beyond him and he turned more and more to the bottle for relief. There were many days when the volunteers would turn up for work to find the doors of the hospital shut. They might see the children peering out of the windows in the middle of the day, unable to get out because Dr Oprea was sleeping in after a boozy night. He alone had the keys to all areas of the hospital and he refused to give them to anyone else because he was officially in charge. So the children often went without a change of clothes; meals came at all times of the day. They were dirty and would often sleep through the day and then be fully awake at night, making a horrendous noise which echoed across the silent hills. The grounds were not kept clean; syringes and rubbish were left lying around and provided dangerous playthings for the children. It was a total nightmare. How could any progress be made if the hospital was being managed so chaotically?

Knowing it was essential for the children's welfare, Jahal continually struggled to inject more order into things, but he was fighting a losing battle. Dr Oprea might agree to something one day and the next would have changed his mind. Then the problem escalated suddenly into a frightening crisis. In the early days Jahal had given Dr Oprea some money to build a little lodge by the lake at the top of the valley, so that the children would have a place of their own to which they could go at weekends or whenever anyone was free to take them. But no building was done and when Jahal asked for the money to be returned it was not available. Jahal assumed it had been stashed away or spent on drink. A quarrel ensued, and Jahal threatened to go to the local television station and complain about the fact that the children were being looked after by an alcoholic – who had also appropriated money given for a charitable purpose – and were living in disgraceful conditions.

This was the situation awaiting ten new volunteers (all young university students) and the volunteer director Jeff Saville when they arrived in Romania. They were collected from the airport late in the evening by Sarah, another volunteer who had only been in Remeti for a week. She was driving the Post Office van left behind by the convoy. Returning along the potholed main road in the darkness, she rounded a bend and crashed into an unlit Gypsy cart. The horse was killed and the Gypsy suffered a broken leg. When the police arrived they were all taken to the police station, where Sarah's passport was confiscated. The volunteers arrived at Remeti just before dawn.

A few days later, when they had agreed the amount of compensation to be paid to the Gypsy, Jahal went by himself first to deliver the money, then to the police station to leave the receipt and retrieve Sarah's passport. He then intended to go on to the television station to record an interview about Dr Oprea as he had threatened. He never got there.

On the steps of the police station he was abducted and hustled into a car where two raincoated gentlemen carrying pistols were waiting to escort him. They were driven out beyond the borders into Hungary, where a Hungarian policeman joined them. They then drove across Hungary, Jahal being closely questioned all the time. Jahal became severely frightened as they jabbed their guns into him, lit cigarettes and stubbed them out on his skin. At one point as they were driving through a wood, they stopped the car suddenly and told him to get out and take off his shoes. He thought this was the end. They then enjoyed themselves at his expense for a while, not hitting him but scaring him as they shot the pistols into the ground by his feet.

When they got back into the car they drove into Czechoslovakia and dumped Jahal near a railway station. Exhausted and shocked, he managed to get on a train back to Budapest, where he phoned a very worried Karen. He had been missing for two days and no one had had the slightest idea where he was. Everyone had thought he must have been beaten up by the Gypsies and a full-scale search had been launched, in which the Gypsies themselves eventually took part. Pat, back in England at this point, had been alerted and she had phoned the French and British embassies in Romania; the Securitate had been involved as well.

In the interests of their safety, it was decided that not only Jahal and Karen but all the other volunteers should return immediately to England. This they did, but within a week the volunteers had returned to Remeti, begging or borrowing the money to do so. The mission would go on, come what may. They could not abandon the children. 'Neither could we,' said Pat. 'It was a crunch point.' She goes on:

We felt very responsible for these young volunteers but also very responsible for the children at Remeti whose plight was unbearable without a volunteer presence. We felt very proud of them when they wanted to go back; we would not have asked them to do so but were very grateful when they insisted. I don't think the White Cross itself was in danger of folding, but without the volunteers' courage the children at Remeti would have had an even more uncomfortable time.

As it was ... we were able to use this situation to our benefit. I was able to say to Dr Oros and the authorities that we believed that Dr Oprea was behind the abduction in some way (he was certainly strutting around the village implying that he was). We were also able to say that the money given him had disappeared and that he could not be trusted as head of the hospital. We also let it be known that if he were not replaced very soon indeed we would cut off all aid to the spital and let the world know why.

Dr Oprea lost his job within two months. Unfortunately he is a very sorry man now – a total alcoholic who is very weepy. We all feel sad for him.

After Dr Oprea was sacked by the authorities at Oradea, he was replaced in Remeti by Dr Marianna Andro, an excellent and caring doctor who is still with the children and loves them all dearly.

Jahal and Karen stayed in England, with Jahal working as the White Cross Mission manager in Truro. He did not return to Romania for at least a year and even after this time he felt some trepidation. He had heard stories that Dr Oprea had been strutting about saying, 'Jahal will be too frightened ever to come back here again. He knows what will happen if he tries to cross me! I'm powerful in Romania; Jahal is just a piece of dirt and he'll be too frightened ever to come back.' Jahal did go back however, though this time accompanied by a minder called Bernie, a big, powerful man, broad and well over six feet tall, well equipped to be a bodyguard.

Jahal did not stay in Romania for long after his return. Graham Banks was appointed field manager in his place, though often worked *in absentia* as he still had a full-time job in Truro. He came out when he could during his holidays. Colin Woodcock, who had just taken a degree in psychology at Plymouth University, took charge on site and according to Graham did a splendid job. Graham indeed pays generous tribute to every volunteer and coordinator with whom he worked. He is always particularly grateful to his 'secret weapon': his translator Maria.

By the summer of 1992 tangible progress had been made in many areas and it became possible to be a little more adventurous with some of the children. During that and the following summer the volunteers and children had a marvellous time with some special holiday programmes. They organized projects on the themes of Giants and Red Indians. Cardboard figures were cut out, music and songs were invented, stories were told and the children danced and sang. A great deal of fun was had by all.

A little exercise in socialization for the children had also been started by this time. The volunteers would take a few of them now and again for a walk to the village 'bar' or cafe for a soft drink or a croissant. This was not a lesson in etiquette or how to behave in public. It was more a way of helping them to feel comfortable in such situations and part of the village community. Susan Rule, one of the volunteers, wrote the following account of a visit to 'The Cafe Bar – Salon 6 Style' which captures the atmosphere of such expeditions beautifully.

Izabella, usually reluctant to leave Salon 6, showed great excitement at the sight of her coat. She knew that a great treat was in store for her.

Yes, it was all girls together for a trip to the social centre of Remeti – the Cafe Bar. Shrill cries of 'apa' [water] filled the air as Erzi approached in her prim pink coat and Eszther, in an unusual burst of energy, followed closely behind. Once seated at the table outside the bar the girls behaved perfectly. Erzi sat with her hands delicately on her knee while Izabella sat still, concentrating on drinking her Fanta. Eszther enjoyed her Fanta immensely and refused to believe that she had drunk all the contents of her bottle, so continued to hold it to her mouth. When she eventually accepted that she had finished every drop we took the girls on a walk to the river. Izabella with perfect aim threw sticks into the river while Eszther posed for photographs. Erzi seemed to have unbounded energy as she ran up and down the pathway and wanted to be spun around again and again.

The next day was the boys' turn. Remus, Stefan and Ioska Silagi left the spital with the same air of excitement as the girls. As we sat outside the bar again Stefan proved that old habits die hard, as every passer by was subjected to his cries of 'mahar' (Gypsy language) as he begged for bread. He also took the opportunity to eat an apple from a ditch. We anticipated much gratitude for the Fanta we bought for him as he was obviously desperate for some light refreshment, but at the first taste of the fizzy orange his nose wrinkled up and he left his Fanta in preference for the scraps of bread given by the villagers. A similar reaction came from Remus as the bubbles went up his nose. He was also more fascinated by the people going into the Cafe Bar and what was inside than in his drink. We sat enjoying the sunshine for some time while Stefan had one last taste of everyone else's drinks just in case he found one that was acceptable to his distinguished palate and the Sherlock Holmes of Remeti – Remus – inspected his empty bottle from every angle. This was followed by the customary climb through someone's window. Once sat down by the river Ioska enjoyed the smells and sounds of the mountain and Stefan enjoyed the tastes.

These visits to the Cafe Bar were carried out throughout the weeks for all the Salon 6 children and will continue to be done. When Lolo helped a volunteer take the bottles back into the cafe another Fanta was bought for him by a villager.

By socializing in their own village the children have the opportunity to be seen and accepted by the local people and to enjoy experiencing the outside world.

For some time Graham Banks had felt that his vocation directed him towards Romania. He believed he should be there, at least for a time, on a permanent basis. If God was calling him, He was also prompting Graham to do something about it himself. So during 1992 and 1993 he wrote between two and three hundred letters to various charities asking for financial contributions as he had to support a family and repay a mortgage. Not one was prepared to help him – Romania was out of their orbit. Despite this setback, and having by now a clear view of his future for the next two or three years, Graham worked hard on preparing a new, improved training programme for the volunteers and an even more detailed one for the Romanian staff.

It had been the intention of the White Cross Mission, almost from the beginning, to hand over the care of the children to the Romanians. It is preferable for children to be brought up by those of their own land, culture and language. Although some of the children could not speak Romanian and under-stood only a little, this was the language which they would hear for the rest of their lives. It was important that those looking after them could speak it properly, which the English volunteers, try as they might, could not.

By the summer of 1994 Graham and Pat had agreed that it really would be best if he could go out as full-time manager. Jahal had by now moved on to work for another charity and the small salary which had been given to him could be transferred to Graham. So he took the plunge, resigned his well-paid job in Cornwall, travelled to Romania and settled into the Woodhouse.

Graham's method of training was down to earth, combining theory with practical skills. In his own words, writing shortly after his arrival as full-time manager based in Remeti:

I have just started a formal staff training programme – 'Working together', which has been
designed to take place and run alongside the
volunteer programme. This programme has
two elements – 'Theory' and 'Practice' – for two
hours in the morning with children with severe
developmental delay/learning and two hours in
the afternoon with a cross section of other children. The thrust of the programme on one
hand is to give the skills of empowering/improv-
ing their own present knowledge, and on the
other hand practical guided experience and
support. All of which has to be sensitively mea-
sured against the time staff are able to offer the
children. This is an important balance as it
would be soul destroying for them to gain
information that could not be implemented.

Quite apart from his vital training work, it is clear from what the volunteers said and wrote about him that Graham made a great contribution to the atmosphere and spirit of the orphanages at Remeti, Bratca and indeed at Oradea, where he offered his training programme to the psychologists and psychiatrists at Spital 6, the neuro-psychiatric hospital. One volunteer writes quite simply:

> I can't finish this short report without mentioning Graham – I think he is a wonderful man, the children obviously adore him and he does such a good job with the volunteers too – he helps us build on our strengths and also look at our weaknesses in a positive way. (Ginny)

Another comments on the progress of Graham's training programme for the Romanian 'educators', the local staff working as paid (but unqualified) teachers:

> Our educators here at Remeti have been working for a month and a half now so I thought I'd write an update on their progress. Well the news is very good, we are very lucky; Florentina, Livia, Simona and Florin are excellent. They have four children each and the children have come on a great deal even in this short time. Children who never spoke are saying words, children who said only words are now having conversations.

The affection these ladies have for even their most trying children is obvious and this together with the new programme of care that they have worked out with Graham is improving the quality of life for the kids a hundred fold.

Relationships between the educators and the volunteers are improving all the time, obviously the language barrier limits us but we are trying and seem to be improving and when it comes down to it and we're all together we're like a group of girls anywhere…

They regarded Graham as the 'big boss man' and he only had to walk into the room and they pretty much stood to attention, but things have got a lot better and they realize he's not anyone to be frightened of, in fact Simona spends all the time they are together correcting his Romanian…

So it's very good news and I for one feel that we are handing the children over into very good hands. (Claudine)

It was Graham who also encouraged the volunteers to write articles, letters and poems in which their reactions and feelings could be expressed. These are published in a little quarterly magazine called *The Gazette*. They are artless and lovely; some are funny, many are moving, all offer a unique perspective on the work from those most closely involved. A selection of these writings is included in Appendix A on pages 194–207.

Graham pays special tribute to the work of the coordinators, who helped him while he was in Romania and organized everything when he was not. The role of coordinator evolved naturally from the presence of particular volunteers who emerged as having obvious organizational skills. Provided that they could stay out in Romania long enough to do so (generally three or four months, although some stayed longer), they were able to take responsibility for the smooth running of one of the orphanages, thus allowing Graham more freedom for strategic planning and training.

By August 1996 Graham had done his best to train the Romanian staff at both orphanages and some of the girls were directly employed by the White Cross as educators. Even so, both hospitals were and still are extremely understaffed, and volunteers are always needed to work alongside the educators.

Over the last few years Graham had achieved an immense amount, giving the task all his energy. Now, in 1996, he was extremely tired and felt it was the right time to return home. Pat paid a final tribute to him in her August 1996 newsletter to all White Cross supporters:

Graham Banks completes his contract with us this September and after two years of wonderful work he is now looking for a new job. I feel

I must tell you all just what an amazing job he
has done. For two years now he has directed
our work, supported our volunteers, cajoled
and persuaded the Romanian staff, walked
hundreds of miles, lived in primitive conditions, suffered insults with a smile and generally stood in for all of us back home. His presence
has made all the difference. One hundred and
seventy four lives made better in every way
because of him. I know he will say that he is
only one cog in a large wheel but on behalf of
all the other cogs, particularly the Directors
and the volunteers, I would like to say a heart
felt THANK YOU! Thank you Graham, you've
been great. We'll miss you!

5

Meet the volunteers

Pat had intended from the beginning that the child-care volunteer programme should help not only the Romanian staff and the children but also the volunteers themselves. Her hope was that going out to Romania to work with these terribly damaged youngsters would help the volunteers find their right direction in life, provide valuable new experiences and reveal hitherto undiscovered emotions. Her hopes were fulfilled, and many of the five hundred volunteers (from all walks of life, some young, some old) who have so far worked at Remeti and Bratca have found the experience a turning point in their lives.

So many people have now taken part in the White Cross work in Romania that it would be impossible to mention them all by name and in detail. Each individual's contribution to the life of the orphanages and to the children who live there has been very special, however, and most volunteers would probably say that they have gained as much as they gave, if not more, from the time they spent there. The stories of the individuals mentioned in this chapter are representative of the effect which the 'White Cross' experience had on all those involved. Taken out of familiar surroundings and faced with children suffering in a way none of them could previously have imagined, the volunteers found themselves challenged, physically, intellectually and emotionally. Many of them seemed surprised to discover personal strengths which enabled them to cope with these challenges, and most felt a deep sense of satisfaction at what they achieved in the short months of their visit. It is true to say that it is not just those on the receiving end of compassion and aid who benefit: those who give wholeheartedly to such ventures gain just as much in a different way.

One volunteer who is well remembered is Nick. He had been in the Forces but had no academic qualifications, and recently had had no sense of direction at all. But after he had been out in Romania for a while he returned home determined to put his life in order. He enrolled on an A Level course, went on to university and is now a fully fledged archaeologist working mainly in Greece. He had talked in Romania about doing such work as if it were an impossible dream; but somehow he made it happen. He was a most resourceful character. If anything needed fixing or mending he would come up with an instant idea about how it could be done. Once he was driving an old Lada from Remeti to Bratca along the river road;

the car hit a rock and cracked the sump. At once he got out, saw what had happened, handed each passenger a piece of chewing gum and said, 'Chew,' which they obediently did. He then filled the crack with chewing gum and the old Lada continued on its journey. He had a quick brain and a wonderful sense of fun. There were moments when he was an absolute star, and no doubt he still is in the archaeological field.

Matt was another great character. At the very beginning, when the search for the first volunteers was on, he went into Pat's office. 'I'm a qualified engineer; just finished in fact. And I'd like to go out to Romania. Could I be of use?' She explained the sort of work he would be doing. 'Yes, that's fine. No problem.'

'Why don't we fill in the forms now?'

'Oh, I haven't got time to do that now. I'm off to Bisley. I'm part of the Cornwall team and I've got to shoot. I'll make an appointment when the match is over and come and see you again.'

A week later Pat was in her study. The phone rang. 'Hello. It's Matt.' She opened her engagement diary.

'Ah, you want to come and see me.'

'Not at the moment. I'm at Gatwick.'

'Gatwick?'

'Yes, I'm on my way to Romania.'

'Romania? but we haven't … you haven't…?'

'What I want to know is – when I get to Romania whom do I speak to? And how do I get to Remeti?'

'Wait a minute. You have to fill in several forms. There are all sorts of things to sort out; you need a police check and an identity card – you need vaccinations and so on. You can't just go.'

'Well I must in a few minutes. I've got my ticket and the plane's due to leave in half an hour. I'll get on out there and when you come out next we'll sort everything out then.'

There was nothing Pat could do but say 'Bon Voyage', but she was concerned that this young man was going out relatively unchecked and unbriefed. As it happened, she was going out herself in two or three weeks' time. Matt had by then arrived at Remeti, settled in and introduced himself as a volunteer. When she arrived, he greeted her happily, and took her on a tour of the hospital almost as if she had never seen it before. He felt himself an old hand.

He took Pat up to the top floor where some of the severely handicapped children lived. They were no longer restricted, but still sitting in their cots, many unable to walk. Just as they walked in, Ardilene, a lad of twelve or thirteen, half stood up in a bit of a crouch, pulled his trousers down and went to the toilet in his cot. Matt had gone ahead into the room and cried out, 'Ugh – how disgusting!'

Pat said calmly, 'Yes, I think you'll find many of them do it. But that's an improvement for Ardilene because at least he doesn't want it to happen inside his pyjamas now. And he's pulled his pyjamas down.

So that really is a step up.'

Matt said, 'What do we do about it?'

'Well since you're in charge of the room old chap – you just said you were – you'll have to clean it up. Go and get some rubber gloves and lots of tissue paper, take it away and just put it in the toilet.' He went – rather slowly – and certainly didn't rush to do this distasteful job, probably hoping that one of the nurses might have it done before he came back. As Pat moved on to the next ward she met Matt coming slowly back with a bowl of water and rubber gloves. A look of horror appeared on his face as he saw how Ardilene had used the interval. Objecting to the large lump of mess left in his cot, he had amused himself by getting rid of it – flinging it all over the room. So poor Matt now had an enormous job to do cleaning it off wherever it had landed. Next time he was no doubt wiser and quicker!

Matt turned out to be one of the most colourful and willing volunteers. He spent hours with Dinu, coaxing him out from under his blanket, getting him to show a little interest in life and to gain some confidence. It was Matt who first got Dinu to walk.

Although Matt was a volatile character, he had a great sense of justice. In the early days some of the Romanian staff tended to hit out at the children, largely because of their own frustration at the situation which had been presented to them. The whole village was bewildered by it all: the sudden influx of children to the orphanage was upsetting, and even the arrival of the White Cross personnel to help caused consternation in some circles. But Matt did what he could to protect the children from the effects of this frustration.

There lived in the village a certain Mrs C., wife of the manager of the construction company, which was quite powerful since it employed about one hundred families in the village. Sadly Mrs C. appeared to be extremely allergic to handicapped and Gypsy children and was horrified whenever she saw them out in the streets of the village. She would make a great fuss and force them to go back to the spital. She particularly objected to them paddling and swimming in the river. *She* swam in that river herself and did not want to swim in water which had been contaminated by 'those' children. So she would very shrilly and angrily order the volunteers to take them downstream of her. Most of the time she was unnecessarily nasty and antagonistic. A further objection was that some of the volunteers were living in a flat (the 'English house') in a building belonging to her husband's company. She nagged him constantly to have them removed. Unfortunately it was Matt who added strength to her voice.

He was taking a walk with a couple of other volunteers when some of the village children taunted them. 'Handicap! Handicap!' they shouted. Matt and his friends ignored the children until they began to throw stones, and one female volunteer was hit. At that Matt aped a monster and in mock fury bounded after the now frightened children. One, as he ran off screaming, fell over. Matt picked him up, shook him and said, 'Don't you ever do that again!'

Unfortunately the boy was Mrs C.'s beloved son. She was so furious that she was determined that the White Cross Mission would leave the village at once. Luckily her husband was more reasonable and in any case he had no authority to remove the Mission from the hospital. He did insist, however, that the volunteers had to leave the flat; and that Matt must leave the village, otherwise the police would arrest him for assault. So, diplomatically, Matt moved to Bratca.

When Matt eventually returned to England, he joined the United Nations and moved on to Sarajevo where he spent some time counselling rape victims; apparently he has been a tower of strength to them too. So a boy who had done an engineering degree with the full intention of finding some appropriate job and settling for that, heard about the need in Romania and responded to it, thereby changing his life completely.

In 1991 James Leslie graduated from Exeter University with a Physics degree. During the following year he spent six months travelling round India with three friends. He still had not discovered what he really wanted to do with his life. One day he phoned Rod

Toms, the teacher of a course on Judo and Akido which he had been taking. By chance Rod's wife Kay (sponsorship secretary for the White Cross) answered the phone, had a chat with James and suggested he might go to Romania as a volunteer with the White Cross Mission. She must have been very persuasive, for he decided to go.

James had no special knowledge of or interest in children and he did not know what to expect. He met the children in Salon 6 first and it was a lovely experience for him. 'They were so open and accepting, welcoming.' He particularly enjoyed rough and tumble with the older ones. Once he was back in England after his stint at Remeti, he completely surprised himself by bursting into tears at the thought of the children he had left behind. He missed them painfully and needed to go back. So he did, for a further three months. One vivid impression James took away with him was that Christmas in Romania was real and meaningful, but back in England it seemed by comparison 'horrible' and commercialized.

When he returned home after his second visit he felt strongly that he would like to work with children permanently, so in 1995 he went to St Mark and St John Teaching College in Plymouth to study for a PGCE. He did not feel right in an ordinary teaching situation, however; it seemed more like management than communication. So he dropped out of the course. Now he has found his real niche in life at a very special school in Lancashire. There are fourteen students at Beech Tree School in Bamber Bridge, Preston, aged from seven to seventeen, and everything is on a one-to-one basis. The stated aims of the school are:

> To provide safety, enjoyment, emotional support, and individual remedial programmes for children whose learning disabilities are compounded by challenging behaviour … To work towards equipping each child with the behaviour and skills for normal living … Communication by whatever means is considered of paramount importance.

James has an innately sensitive and gentle nature, and he loves these troubled children. There is no doubt in his mind that his time in Romania had a deep influence in determining the direction of his life. He is also convinced that someone like Dinu would be immensely helped by such intensive, full-time care.

Christy Piper is James's girlfriend. She had just finished her A Levels and had already applied to do voluntary work when she met James, just before he went to Romania for the first time. When she is teased that she only went to Romania to be with him, she agrees that this was an incentive but not her only motive.

Below left: Dinu, the 'Blanket Boy'

Left: Mike, the policeman, lifts children down from the lorry on their first ever picnic trip to the lake.

Below right: Some children at Bratca

Middle left: Children at Remeti allowed out in the streets to play at snowballs with the village children

Top left: The village of Remeti

Bottom left: Jeff Townsend with Stuart Renfree, July 1991

Left: Magnificent maintenance men and women

Below: Pat with Ian Stirling of West Country TV at the Cornwall County Show, 1993.

Bottom: The children at 'Casa Fericita' – at home!

Below: Camelia spends her life in her cot, as she has epilepsy and it is difficult to get her medication right.

Right: Occasionally the volunteers can get Camelia out into the sun.

Bottom left: The orphanage at Remeti

Bottom right: The new hospital at Bratca

Far right: The volunteers who worked through the summer of 1996 to get 'Casa Fericita' ready for the children.

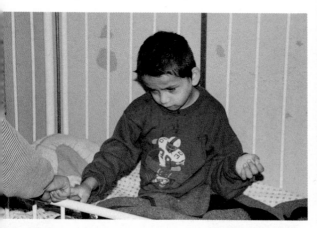

Below: The children at Remeti at educational play.

Right: Pat fundraising at a garden fete.

Top right: Viorel, Elena and Erika

Middle right: Spital at Remeti, Easter 1997

Bottom right: Soakaway at the Woodhouse – Jeff Townsend with Chris, watched by Ilyana's son

Top: Summer production of 'Giants'

Above: Painting session

It happened that when they reached Romania, the first time she met the Remeti children was on a train from Bucharest. They were returning from the great concert of 1994, given in honour of the visit from the Suffragan Bishop of Truro and the British Ambassador (but more of this later). Christy had already met disabled and autistic people and although she was apprehensive about meeting the Salon 6 children she found she was interested rather than shocked. In fact, she preferred being with them than with the less disturbed children, and she felt she was able to help them more. One of her main difficulties was that she found the cramped conditions of the Woodhouse difficult.

She remembers once that when she was out walking with a group of children, Gusti, one of the boys, fell into the canal. He was not in any real danger and only hurt his head a little. But Christi cried. 'Why do you cry?' the children said. Doubtless they had all endured so much that a harmless accident was nothing. But Christy is a highly sensitive person. She was brought up as an Anglo-Catholic though her parents divorced when she was seven. She feels that institutionalized religion is not for her. What is important is that the spirit of love and compassion abroad in the universe reaches everyone, and gains new power from each person it inspires. 'We are all here to help each other as much as we can.' She is now at university reading a combination of Japanese and deaf studies, as the Japanese are advanced in their understanding and treatment of deafness.

Alan Woodburn is a typical untypical volunteer. A happily married man with two teenage children, a degree in Physics and Philosophy and a considerable talent for writing, Alan went to Romania out of sheer desperation. He was unable to find a publisher for the two or three books he had written and was feeling very depressed because he had no job. He heard that the White Cross Mission needed volunteers and decided to apply. He would have been equally willing to help any victims of what he calls 'this cruel and tragic world' if he had a chance. Had he been religious he would most probably have believed that God had directed him to Remeti, for the experience was rewarding. But Alan is an atheist with a highly analytical, rational – and sometimes acerbic – mind. It was almost in a mood of rebellion that he decided to do something irrational like going to Romania.

Although he felt great compassion for the children and like all the volunteers gave them support and love, his distinctive contribution was in the sphere of music. His main instrument, though he is not a professional, is the guitar. Indeed he went busking in the centre of Truro to help raise money for his expenses. In an unpublished manuscript which he has written about his time at Remeti he describes how he tried to make music and sounds come alive for the children:

Ioan was one of the first Salon 6 children I'd met, and his story was particularly tragic though not at all typical. He'd been a healthy child, living with his family, until he caught meningitis. This left him both brain damaged and epileptic. The only solution Romania could afford to control his fits was to keep him constantly drugged on phenobarbitone. What little faculties were left to him after the brain damage were thus further depressed by the drugs and he lived a puzzled far away existence, his awareness stirred only occasionally by memories of his past. One of the triggers guaranteed to prompt such memories was the appearance of any strange adult. His constant, confused hope was that it would be one of his parents. They'd been unable to cope with him at home and had put him into institutional care. Most confusingly of all, they still visited occasionally, and so gave him some expectation that the stranger might indeed be his mother or father. When I'd first encountered Ioan, I'd been with Jay – the fierily alternative but gently affectionate young man from whom I took over the 'music' slot on the programme. Ioan's first response to me was to tilt his head, look somehow simultaneously bewildered and hopeful, widen his eyes, and mouth '*Tata?*' at me.

'He's asking if you're his father,' said Jay.

'Help. What do I say?'

'Not much you can say,' said Jay, stroking Ioan's head soothingly.

The rewarding thing about Ioan was his response to music. His normally miserable countenance would light up magically at the clumsiest attempt at a tune, and he would clap along, his face distended in a rictus of glee, as joyous as it had once been wretched. He was quite good, too, at holding fairly complex rhythms with a tambourine or indeed anything I handed him, whilst I played along with the guitar or sang.

Sessions with him were indulgent ones – it was enough to witness such unaccustomed happiness for half an hour and not worry too much if he was actually making any progress. But every so often, even when we were well used to each other, in mid tune, his face would suddenly cloud, as if he'd heard a distant sound – a voice from his past. His head would incline quizzically and he'd stare at me, grab my hand and brush it to his cheek: '*Tata?*' imploring me to answer 'Yes'.

'*Nu. Nu Tata. Alan. Tata nu este aici.*' Daddy isn't here.

I would watch him struggling to take in that, no, I was only Alan, and soon, after strumming a few more chords, he would light up again and we would continue.

Alan was disappointed, however, that during his first visit he had not been very successful in getting the children to sing songs:

But it was too late. I was leaving, frustrated at not having got together any real music on my first visit. Once home, I scoured every available source for details of Romanian children's songs, but drew blanks, except from my family contacts Tom and Camelia in Cluj. They sent some photocopied sheets, and things began to look more promising. I decided that when I went to Romania for the second time I would pay them a visit before I started work. It proved a very fruitful acquaintance.

Whilst staying there, I arranged to visit the Cluj Blind School, also through a family contact. Having already seen what the Romanians thought of their handicapped Gypsy orphans, my hopes for the Blind School were not great. My contact was one Elena Bucur, and I could already see her – a burly uniformed elephant of a woman, probably carrying a stick. But she was quite other. I arrived at the school and found myself with this pleasant and rather beautiful young woman who talked to the children in a voice of exceptional kindness and calm. Her class was a small one, and an awful lot of them reminded me of children I already knew in Remeti, though there was no particular Gypsy bias in this school population. Her class sang me some songs, without any hint of either inhibition or coercion, and then we toured the school where other classes gladly interrupted their lessons to do performances for me.

It was Elena, though, who gave me the songs I really needed to start work in Remeti. There were plenty that I subsequently used, but chief amongst them was '*Un Elefant*', and really I should have picked it up before. Oh, the curses that have rained upon that song from volunteers forced to suffer it...

Un Elefant se legana
Pe o panza de paianjen
Si fiindca ea nu se rupea
A mai chemat un elefant
UNO, DOI, TREI, PATRU, CINCI, SASE,
SAPTE, OPT, NOUA, ZECE.

It was a counting rhyme. It meant:

One elephant was swinging
On a spider's web
And because it wasn't breaking
Called for another elephant

And then it built up to ten. When ten elephants were on the web, it finally broke, as you might well guess, and to the relief of all volunteers. I knew little what I was starting.

It wasn't that songs were the core of my Remeti work. Since I worked mostly with Salon 6, auditory awareness was more the thing. The chief aim was to get some response to any kind of sound, musical or otherwise. With some children it never happened. I banged instruments, strummed the guitar, played tapes or sang, and Olizen would merely smile, regurgitate thoughtfully, swallow it, and approach me for a piggyback or whizzy. He showed no interest in using any of the instruments himself, and really would rather have been somewhere else. Often, so would I.

Other children, though not interested in music as such, liked to play with sound. They could make funny noises on the guitar by scraping up the strings, or wave chime bars round their heads. I saw a gap in resources here, and felt sure I could do better things. After my first visit I went on some courses, the chief practical outcome of which was my blessed discovery of transducers. A transducer is just the guts of a simple microphone. It can be had for 30p, and, stuck on to any object with Blutack and fed into an amplifier (in this case a half broken radio/cassette), will take the tiny vibrations and make them into big noises. This was magic. Stefan had mostly contented himself with picking small stones or bits of grit off the carpet and dropping them on to a tambourine, whilst sucking his thumb. Stefan was one of our most deeply damaged children, though he hadn't come from Cadea. He'd been a Gypsy street-child in Oradea, when a car accident left him in hospital. Nobody came to claim him, and even the name Stefan was made up by staff. Traumatized by the accident, or by his earlier life, he never spoke sensibly and spent his days defending himself against the blows he always expected. This marked him out as a victim, and a lot of the children and staff responded by treating him as one, further compounding the earlier damage. He was rarely without bruises. The little he did speak was often Gypsy (Romany – quite distinct from Romanian) or Hungarian, though he was beginning to prattle in disjointed Romanian – more a reporting of his inner mental life than anything resembling communication.

Now I fitted the tambourine with a transducer. The rattle of falling grit became an immense sound, and he looked up, suddenly and
momentarily aware of the outside world. Other
children used the device to scrape along walls,
on the guitar strings or over their hair or faces,
exploring the different sounds each made. It
was a great toy.

The amplifying equipment I'd put together
for the transducer also worked with a microphone. This was a boon for some children.
Though my activity was 'Muzica', I always felt a
responsibility to work on speech as well. I had
the right equipment, and I spoke Romanian
fairly well. It was hard to persuade any child
that, just because I was babbling 'Ga ga ga' at
them, there was any great payoff for them in
copying me. But the microphone changed that.
Suddenly 'Ga ga ga' became a huge and exciting
thing to say, when booming out through the
amplifier. And when we'd got the basic speech
sounds going, it was only a small step to get
them to say a real word, always in a relevant
context. It was one of the areas in which I really
felt the children made progress during my time.
There are few things more exciting than hearing a child using, perhaps for the first time in
fourteen years of life, a word with its proper
meaning – perhaps asking for water: '*apa*', or

saying that they're finished doing something: '*gata*', or best of all addressing you by name. And though I couldn't take credit for it, I was elated when Stefan, who had no Romanian when I first met him, came out with a whole sentence. He was anxious to get out of the Salon 6 door which was barred by a bent nail at the top: '*Deschide usa acolo sus!*' – open the door up there.

Alan tried hard to master the Romanian language and to help the volunteers and children to do so. He feels strongly that real communication and understanding is dependent not only on empathy and body language but on verbal language too. He is now learning Polish and has embarked on a course teaching English to foreign students in Poland. But the most important effect on himself that the experience at Remeti has had, he says, is that he is now far more understanding of and empathetic with any kind of handicap.

Roger Hamer is a pharmacist, now verging on retirement. He had never been overly enthusiastic about the White Cross Mission and first went mainly to accompany his wife, Jill. Now it has taken him over; he is as smitten with the whole project as he is with one of its little characters, Adrian. He writes:

I first saw Adrian sitting in Salon 6 in his place, third from the door. He gives a wicked little smile and toddles over.

Our first outing was a walk in the snow in tandem with Erzi. He was really hard work as his walking isn't good and his desire to remove his boots at the first opportunity doesn't help. As soon as we turn round to come back he starts to play up, dragging his boots off, shrieking, sitting down, but always with that mischievous grin. I end up having to carry him the last 200 metres. I'm shocked at the way a group of village children go out of their way to snowball him even though he's helpless in my arms. These children are accompanied by their mother who says nothing!

A session in the creative play room with Jill and I is mayhem. He throws sand, paint, water and tantrums in equal amounts – half an hour is more than enough so we take him to the sensory room where he sits wrapped in my arms like an angel looking up at me and smiling.

I haven't realized how much Adrian has grown on me. Today when I collect him he gives me a fabulous smile when I call his name and climbs into my arms in a flash, hugs my head so tight that I can hardly see (I learnt on the first day that contact lenses instead of glasses are essential for Salon 6).

We go down to educational play and he sets to work studiously disassembling Lego houses that Erzi has patiently had me build for an hour. He is very positive in taking it apart, not destructive, each individual block has to be separated and placed in the box. Placed is perhaps a little too gentle a way to describe the action but the blocks do end up in the box!

It is difficult to describe how I feel about Adrian. It started with shock, this further enhanced when I find out this child the size of a six year old is nearly fifteen. The shock turns to horror when some of his tantrums are seen at first but within days I now find him irresistible. His faith in me carrying him downstairs when he launches himself into the void given the least amount of support, is astonishing. The glee in his eyes when I call his name and when I chase him down the corridor, (yes he can run when he has a mind to) the hugs when carrying him upstairs – the list goes on. I'm only sorry that the chance of getting him to sit still in my rucksack for twenty-four hours will prevent me kidnapping him when we come to leave.

Hannah Whale was manageress of a hairdressing salon in a shop owned by her parents. She had often thought about doing some voluntary work but somehow hesitated; until in 1994 she applied to go to

Romania and in July of that year found herself at Bratca, the 'sister' orphanage to Remeti since 1992. It then had only twenty-four children, housed in cramped conditions in a disused hospital which was old and dirty. The first two volunteers had quite adequate accommodation, however, and the atmosphere of the place was fine. The orphanage is some way away from the village, in beautiful grounds, and this seclusion, together with the smaller number of children, means that from the beginning the villagers have felt less threatened than they were at first at Remeti. They have always been friendly and supportive and the brighter children have been allowed to attend the village school. Bratca Hospital is understaffed, and although the doctor in charge, Dr Liana, remains charming and gentle, she is, being responsible for the hospital, the orphanage and the clinic in the village, dreadfully overworked.

The Dutch had been for some time financing the building of a new orphanage in the grounds and everyone was looking forward to its opening. Especially as the coal and wood fires in the original building gave off smoke and fumes, making the orphanage unavoidably grubby and causing the children to suffer from coughs and bronchial troubles.

The air was rather better in the summer of 1994, when Hannah arrived. She was taken first of all to see the children in Salon 4 (comparable to Salon 6 at Remeti) and she admits she was shocked. She had never seen such 'damaged' children before. But she got on well with them. She returned to Cornwall in September, went to tell Pat of her experiences, and was persuaded to go out again. In December she returned to Bratca as the sole volunteer. By then the number of children at the spital had risen to thirty-two with the arrival of six girls from Tinka, 'whose behaviour,' as Hannah wrote at the time, 'can only be described as like that of little wild animals – with, thankfully, the emphasis on the little'.

Come 1995, Hannah was asked to stay on as coordinator, which she describes as 'the supporting of the volunteers both in and out of the spital and to help them to understand the culture of Romania. And most important to design programmes for the children which the volunteers could implement.'

One big problem she faced was the lack of activity rooms for the children at Bratca during the winter. In the summer they could work outside. Perhaps the new, Dutch-built hospital would help? She well remembers its official opening, which coincided with the arrival of its new inhabitants, thirty-two children from the hospital at Nucet:

They arrived in three Volkswagen vans and I distinctly remember them being dressed in matching Hawaiian shirts and shorts. It was mayhem. The official opening of the Spital had, for some reason, been organised for the same day. The local dignitaries were all there, and they had a slap up meal inside, while the children sat around on blankets waiting for theirs, and having already endured a three and a half to four hour journey, you can imagine what the atmosphere was like. In fact I was punched in the mouth by a girl who was knee high to a grasshopper and Philip had his leg bitten.

Unfortunately the new building did not include activity rooms so Hannah had to draw up programmes for over sixty children, twenty of whom were 'Salon 4' cases, without the proper space in which to work with them. The summer was not so bad, because the volunteers were plentiful – there were eleven of them – and they could work outside with the children. The winter months proved more difficult, in spite of the arrival of portacabins from England, but somehow Hannah and the rest struggled resourcefully through.

At the end of her time in Romania, Hannah wrote:

I thank Mama Pat for making it possible for me to have had my experience, also my thanks to Philip who was and still is a good friend and partner in crime, and lastly, to Graham who stuck by me through thick and thin, I couldn't have done it without him. He was my anchorman. He still is one of my best friends and I am forever in his debt.

My job as co-ordinator was a good one. It gave me the chance to meet a lot of very sound people which I might not have done in normal circumstances. The relationships you form in Romania can often be quite intense, due to the situation. A lot of support is given by many, and when the emotions run high or low you get through them to face another day. I just hope I was able to support and help others as they did me.

Juliet Rowe gave herself the best birthday present she could ever have had when she set out for Romania on 28 June 1995. She had obtained A Levels in History, English and Classical Studies at Camborne Community College. All her friends seemed to be off abroad somewhere so she followed the fashion, taking an *au pair* job in Florida. It was a pleasant and maturing experience. She felt a little nervous, but is grateful for the way the Americans prepared her for her year as an au pair, particularly for the well-planned introduction run by an organization based at Greenwich, Connecticut. 'They really held my hand.' It gave her the confidence which otherwise she might not have had, to later travel abroad on her own.

When she returned to England she decided she would like to do some voluntary work while she was waiting to start her college course the following September in Theology and Religious Studies at St

Mary's, Twickenham. She applied to the Red Cross, but was disappointed, for they required more experience and qualifications than she had. Hearing about the White Cross Mission on local radio, she applied to them, and this time was warmly welcomed. Her first stay was short, just from June to September 1995. She was not sure what to expect and so tried to prepare her attitude beforehand, making herself ready to control any reaction of shock or horror. And she did, although she became saddened from time to time as she realized the depth of the deprivation or damage some of the children had suffered.

On her return to England she found she had been truly bitten by the Romanian bug and worked as a catering assistant at the college to earn the money to go back. This time it was for an even shorter period, for three and a half weeks after her exams in January 1996. From February to June she was at college, and thinking seriously about the possibility of giving herself a sort of sabbatical by taking a year off. She approached her tutors somewhat tentatively, but somewhat to her surprise they were most supportive.

While still in England Juliet had been encouraged to take on the role of coordinator at Bratca (to replace Hannah). 'A great thing about Pat is that she gives people an opportunity to prove themselves.' Though if she had known what being a coordinator involved before she went, she doubts whether she would have agreed. But Graham was still around, and he prepared her for the job in a very practical way, introducing her to all the shops and people she might need, and showing her where she must order wood or seek help about electricity. Graham, according to Juliet, was a 'star', 'mad' and 'amazing'. He got to know everyone, and prepared everyone for whatever task they had to perform, giving them little 'psychological confidence-boosting pep ups'. And he had a lovely sense of humour. When Graham left, Juliet felt like bawling, and only just restrained herself. She stayed at Bratca as coordinator for a year, returning to England just once for a holiday in February 1997, then going back until June to finish her 'sabbatical' year away.

She has two large albums full of photos of the children she loves so much. One picture shows Rodika sitting underneath the washbasins, in whose shadow she apparently found some sort of security. Juliet worked with Rodika for three months and at last managed to coax her out of her hiding place.

Has her experience in Romania changed her religious or philosophical attitude to life? It has certainly made her more confident and positive, and given her a tremendous feeling for children, particularly those who are weak and poorly. She had even found herself rejoicing in the joy on the children's faces when they were given jam sandwiches! It has made her question the attitudes of people in general – but not the Romanians in particular. They still believe that an unwanted or handicapped child is likely to be better looked after in an institution than in a family itself severely hampered by poverty.

Juliet was baptized as an Anglican and would call herself a Christian who sometimes attends church. She still has faith in God and in Jesus but is not so sure about the church. She is also not quite sure about the topic of her dissertation, or what career she will follow when she has obtained her degree.

One thing she is absolutely sure of, however, is the invaluable work the White Cross Mission is doing. Everyone – and she insists everyone, including the Directors, the Secretary, every single volunteer, the sponsors, the fundraisers and last, but in no way least, the maintenance men – gives unstintingly. She gives an example of how 'Sir' Jeff (Townsend), the 'Big Boss' maintenance man, once arrived with minibuses of his men to replace a septic tank at the first private house bought by the White Cross. He leapt out, put on overalls and gloves and set to work, dirty work, emptying the cesspit. Her enthusiasm is rhapsodic but entirely sincere. Digging, painting, cleaning out cowsheds – everybody contributes. They're all amazing, she says, 'bloomin' lovely!'

Helen Bray first heard of the White Cross Mission when she was thirteen years old and Pat Robson preached at her church. She did not actually visit Romania, however, until a group of students and two of their teachers went to Remeti in 1996 as part of their NND (Nursery Nurses Diploma) course at Truro College. The course covered the care of children with special needs, but did not deal with such extreme conditions as those suffered by the Romanian children. The group of students stayed only for two weeks but Helen knew she would go again, which she did in January 1997, staying for four months.

She spent time in the first house, 'Casa Fericita', which she described as 'lovely', and the housemother, Claudine, as a 'brilliant mum'. If only there were enough houses for every one of the children who were capable of living away from the hospital.

Helen returned home with some sadness in her heart because she fears for the future of the children in Salon 6 and Salon 4. Some, she thinks, must have been damaged at birth, but others were harmed purely by the terrible trauma of their early lives. She also feels that boredom adds to their problems, and that total one-to-one care, as at James Leslie's school, is probably their only hope of healing.

During the four months at Remeti, Helen learnt a little Romanian and felt happier when able to relate directly to the Romanians. She felt more at home; and she thoroughly enjoyed a short stay with a Romanian family when one maintenance convoy was occupying the Woodhouse.

According to Helen, the maintenance team are so kind to the children, giving them so many trips and treats while they are out there, that the childcare volunteers simply cannot compete with them! But even the children can pay for drinks sometimes. Once when Helen told a group of boys that she was going out for a while to the bar, one of the boys, Deju, became furious, giving her a long diatribe about the evils of alcohol. He must, she thought, have been a victim of its abuse.

'No, I'm going to the bar – the cafe bar, for a Cola.'

At that he relaxed and smiled, put his hand in his pocket and gave her some coins. 'Let me treat you!'

She wondered where he could have found them, but accepted them gracefully and gratefully.

Had her experience strengthened or weakened her faith? Brought up as a Christian and attending traditional family worship at an Anglican church, she had sometimes wondered what it was all really about, though she had never seriously doubted or questioned. The time in Romania, however, had confirmed what she regarded as the essentials of her faith, strengthened by the fact that her own church had enthusiastically sponsored her financially and supported her in other ways too.

Helen is an unusually lovely girl, in appearance and personality. She is warm, natural and friendly and could, no doubt, find a nannying job with a wealthy family and perhaps travel with them and enjoy a luxurious lifestyle. Some nannies do! Now, though, after Romania, her priority is to care for a child, or children, with special needs.

6

The children

'I wish that some of the volunteers, particularly the early ones, could see them now. They would be so pleased and proud knowing that their little efforts – in fact not such little ones – had made such a difference.' Pat describes what a joy and delight it is to go into the orphanages now and to see so many polite, charming children. 'They greet one with smiles and handshakes, you could take them into any restaurant, any society and they would fit in beautifully.' It is now more than six years since Pat first set eyes on the sixty children who had just been transferred from Cadea to Remeti, and whom she remembers as 'really apologies for children, gaunt, haggard creatures, with staring eyes, unable to walk and talk'.

Sadly Pat's glowing description above only includes the main group of able children, not those still in

Salon 6 at Remeti and Salon 4 at Bratca, or the one or two who have fallen by the wayside. Forty of the children now go to their own White Cross Mission school at Remeti or the village school at Bratca, a few have been adopted or are being fostered, and some are living in the houses which the White Cross Mission has bought for them. Pat has been returning regularly every two or three months to keep in personal contact with the Romanian authorities, with those involved in the running of the orphanages, with the volunteers and with the children.

Every child has his or her own dramatic story, though some of the main events and characters in the drama may be hidden for ever. There is no doubt that in the short period since 1991, the influence of the White Cross Mission has been crucial. It has always been beneficial, aiming at the restoration of body, mind and spirit. It has not always been as successful as it longed to be. Even where it has seemed to fail, however, it has not given up the faith that love given can never be lost.

Dinu, 'the blanket boy', is so well known that he has almost become a tragic emblem for the White Cross Mission. He suffered and survived such extreme deprivation and the fact that he has been able to experience any of the normal joys of childhood at all is a tribute to and a symbol of the persistence and love of the volunteers.

When he was taken from his cellar at Cadea the light was too much for him and at Remeti he refused to come out from underneath his blanket for three months. He might peep out, but it took many, many weeks of patient persuasion before he would let anyone invade the security it gave him, and he would make an enormous fuss if anyone wanted to change or clean him. Very gradually, however, Dinu came out into the light, until he recognized that if someone came into his room with a little pair of boots, that meant that he was going somewhere nice. The volunteers might take him down to the river in a wheelchair, where they would encourage him to throw stones. Back in the cot he would pull the blanket right over his head again. But gradually – very gradually – he would pull it back a little further, and then further, and peep from underneath it until it became more like a hood than a tent.

Matt, the young engineer from Cornwall, was one of many who gave Dinu an enormous amount of help and encouragement and by September 1991 he was able to stand up. When Pat next went out in December, he not only offered her a sweet someone had given him but actually walked a few steps. Everyone who had met him was excited and when Pat got back to Truro the news had travelled fast. 'Dinu can walk! Dinu can walk!' Pat's phone was buzzing. Even so, at the age of thirteen he was only the size of an eight-year-old, and could still only make rat noises.

Nevertheless, Dinu had made steady progress and everyone rejoiced.

Sadly, at the time of writing he seems to be slowly regressing. At seventeen he can still walk a little, but has periods when he just keeps hitting his head against a wall, or banging it with his hands, opening up old wounds. The last time Pat saw him he was sitting, with his hands tied, in the middle of a room full of children. The nurse stood in front of him, wanting to shield the sad sight from Pat's view. When she quietly untied one hand, it flew at once to his head and continued to batter it. His condition is desperately sad and uncomfortable, and the way ahead is not clear, particularly as the older he becomes, the more powerful he grows. Neither the nurses nor Dr Marianna have psychiatric experience.

Between the stages of regression Dinu can appear stable and sociable and he has shown interest in painting and music. Nonetheless, his destiny now seems to point to Nucet, the adult mental institution, where he may not receive much loving care, and one is forced to wonder whether this might just seem like a second hell for him.

Josif is the boy who, at the age of four, had cried in his cot at Cadea and been beaten about the head by an older boy and practically blinded. In spite of this, ever since the White Cross Mission first met him at the age of nine, he had always been a smiling child of normal intelligence. When he was eleven he was brought over to England to see a Dorset eye specialist who managed to implant a plastic lens to give him sight in one eye.

He stayed with Pat after the operation, and he was full of happiness, running round with excitement and delight, staring into flowers, pulling out drawers and examining their contents, asking for sunglasses as the light was too bright. When the time came for him to return to Romania, he became sad and quiet. Once back there, however, his only troubles were that he suffered a few headaches and the sun was so bright that the older children loved stealing his sunglasses. Until one day in 1994, in purely harmless play, one of his friends used an empty biro case as a gun and loaded it with little bits of paper. One of them landed in Josif's eye, instantly blinding him. It was a cruel and tragic accident.

At once Pat set in motion all the procedures to get him to England to visit the Dorset surgeon once again. The process is a lengthy one and it has been a long wait. Recently, after months of paperwork and legal wrangling, she has been told that Josif should soon receive a passport. But this has really come too late. He is already totally blind – and is now very sub-dued and quiet, totally unlike the boy who romped round the rectory celebrating his new-found sight. He has to find his way precariously round the orphanage by touch, which could be quite dangerous for him. He has lost the chance of independence, his future is uncertain and it seems he may have to live in a home for the blind.

Horia is a gentle schizophrenic. He hears voices and believes he is an angel; his best friends are Gabriel and Michael and he talks to them as naturally as he would to you and me. He loves to give everyone the low-down on what the angels have been saying. He may be gentle, but his actions can be unnerving, especially for the nurses, and especially if they have been a bit rough with one of the children. They might see Horia lurking in the shadows holding a wooden cross and watching everything that is going on. Suddenly he might say, 'God has told me that the children will go straight to heaven when they die because of the terrible sufferings they're having to put up with down here.' One can imagine what the nurses must feel.

But there is another side to Horia. An uncle turned up one day. He had come, to satisfy the family, to find out how his nephew was. In full police regalia and with a pistol at his belt, he introduced himself to the boy. And Horia, unexpectedly delighted at this image of power, and deciding how much he would like to become a policeman, turned his cross on its side so that it became a gun! However, it soon became his cross again when the novelty had worn off. When he was still at Remeti, before he was moved to Bratca, he was often to be seen up the hill, sitting among the gravestones in the old cemetery chattering to Gabriel and Michael. One worry this inspired was that since be believed he could fly, as they could, he might try to take off from the top of the hill.

He never did attempt to do this, but he was at one point moved to Nucet. Very soon he escaped and made his way across the mountains back to Remeti. Dr Marianna, knowing him to be a gentle, harmless boy, had the good sense to take him in, give him clothes and contact the authorities. They agreed that if he was unlikely to cause any trouble he could stay. A month later Dr Marianna herself moved to Bratca and took Horia with her, where he still is today, and where everyone hopes he will be allowed to stay.

Josca had suffered from polio as a baby, and when he was at Cadea his left leg stuck out at an angle. An Austrian charity arranged for him to have his leg straightened in Vienna. This involved several visits and although the leg was straightened it was still quite a bit shorter than the other, and he never wanted to use it. He preferred his crutches and loved racing round on them. As he refused to put his one foot down, however, the muscles began to atrophy, indeed one doctor forecast that the leg would shrivel.

Josca learnt to speak good English at Remeti, and his German is fluent since he spent three six-month periods in Vienna. He is intelligent, and particularly once he had turned seventeen, being trapped in an institution became very frustrating for him. He had times of violence, particularly against the other children, hitting out at them with his crutches, and they naturally became frightened. So at seventeen-and-a-half he went with Horia to Nucet; and he too ran away and crossed the mountains back to Remeti. It was a more difficult journey for him, because of his leg, so he had to rely on hitching lifts. He arrived at Remeti in the rain, a very pathetic figure dripping wet, standing outside, just wanting to be let inside the orphanage. Dr Marianna, however, felt that she could not ask the authorities to grant permission for Josca to stay. Unlike Horia, he might be a danger to others.

He slept for three nights in a shed in one villager's backyard, and then got a lift to Oradea, where he was given a bed in the hospital. But again he ran away and now lives on the streets, begging. In some ways his situation is not so bad, though it is, of course, far from ideal. He can speak good English and good German, he is charming and personable and he homes in on the tourists who do not feel threatened by him. When Pat saw him last he said he felt free and would refuse to be locked up again. She felt that as he was already quite a hard character, this experience would toughen him further and that he would most probably survive. But how sad that any child, who has received love and care from so many people who have worked so hard to foster his best potential, should have to end up either in a mental hospital or on the streets.

Micki went to Cadea when he was about seven, having previously lived with his family nearby. His father was an alcoholic and his mother schizophrenic, and the house they lived in was run down and rough with an earthen floor and no glass in the windows; food too, was poor and scarce. Their father, in a drunken rage, would often tie Micki and his brother to a tree and beat them. On one occasion Micki was beaten senseless and both boys were taken to hospital. The second time this happened the police asked the boys if they really wanted to return home, and they were given the option of going back to their parents or to the children's home at Cadea. Micki, not knowing what Cadea was like – for he is a very intelligent boy – chose to go there, but his brother chose to return home. Micki has now been adopted, is living in England and doing well. But, intelligent and integrated as he is, he will always have this nagging worry about the fate of his brother. No one yet knows what happened.

Camelia is a gentle child who seems as much a victim of a lack of medical expertise as of epilepsy. No one has been able to achieve the right medication for her. It is either too high – and she becomes a zombie – or too low – and she becomes jerky and uncontrolled. Very rarely does the balance seem correct. Summer is the best time for her; for then she can be taken out of her cot at the Bratca hospital to sit in the sun on a blanket or even go for a walk; for she can walk. Winter is her saddest time. She sits in her cot, usually wet and 'medicated' out of this world, pale faced but always with a smile when someone goes in to see her.

Camelia's plight highlights the urgent need for a doctor who can be devoted only to the children and who could, for example, monitor her medication and spend time getting it right. At present the doctor in charge of the hospital has too heavy a workload. He or she has to look after patients in the hospital and the clinic in the village as well as care for the children in the orphanage.

Another child who is still very much in need is Eszther. When she came from Cadea she was eight years old, a quiet, docile child who could barely move, but who smiled at everyone. Gradually, however, she was encouraged to sit up and with sunken, dark-ringed eyes she looked like a little old lady. Dr Oprea was the doctor in charge in those early days. Eszther would just sit for day after day in her cot; she was wet but was changed only once a day; she did not complain, indeed she could not. Even in the summer she would just sit there, the flies gathering round her mouth and eyes; and in the winter, with such lack of movement, she would be bitterly cold.

Pat remembers going to see her one day for a quick visit at the very beginning of spring. The room had just been cleaned because of the smell and all the windows were open. Eszther was alone and she was blue with cold. Pat called for Dr Oprea and asked for Eszther to be moved to a warmer room and for more blankets to be issued to the children generally. She warned Dr Oprea that she would hold him responsible if Eszther died.

When she got back to England Pat said to Sarah, one of the volunteers, 'When you're out there, whatever else you do please make Eszther your special project. Next time I'd like to see her walking, because if she doesn't walk soon, if she's left neglected in that cot, she will die.' Pat told Sarah how, when she had picked Eszther up out of the cot, she looked like a little two-year-old, although she was eight or nine. Her thin white legs, folded underneath her for so long, just fell uselessly down.

Sarah worked very hard with the little girl, doing all she could to strengthen the weak muscles, and although she needs a lot more help, Eszther is now talking, walking and even running.

No one who has ever been to Remeti could ever forget Bujorel. He is very hyperactive and very cheerful, always wearing a great big grin. Out comes a camera and there is Bujorel's hand, ready to click the control. Or he is in front of the camera making a funny face. You cannot turn around without him being there, the self-appointed clown of the place. When a vehicle arrives there is Bujorel waiting to get in, and he does.

Turn your back and he will be behind the steering wheel. He gets absolutely everywhere, and people used to and still do get very exasperated with him and say, 'Bujorel – go away!'

His hyperactivity may be caused by lack of attention and boredom and he will deliberately do something naughty to attract notice. At school he is a real fidget, but he is intelligent and can concentrate when he is really interested. There are plans, which hopefully can be realized, to settle him in a house where a mechanic is going to be in charge. He could then learn a little, perhaps a lot, about cars, and this would make him the happiest boy in the world.

Gyungi's is perhaps the saddest story of all, because nobody seemed to know anything at all about her. She had been at Oradea and was later transferred to Nucet, to the children's wing of the adult mental hospital. She, with all the others, was sedated every day. When these particular children came to Bratca the sedation was stopped, and they became like wild animals. It was clear from the beginning that Gyungi also suffered quite severely from pains in her abdomen. No one, however, seemed to take much notice of them; the pains were ignored or dismissed. She was a quiet, gentle girl and did not make a fuss or cry: having endured pain for so long she had learnt to suffer without complaining. Then suddenly she was no more. This thin, plain-faced little girl of thirteen died in her sleep, one night in 1996. The volunteers were distraught when her body was taken away to be buried, no one knew where. Later though, her parents were contacted and she was given a proper burial. These are Pat's final words on the sad story:

What a shame that her parents hadn't shown an interest in her while she was alive. We felt badly about Gyungi because hers was our first death in six years. We knew we had failed her, we all had, just by allowing the Romanian authorities who had no interest to have their way. It's Gyungi's death which has made us absolutely determined to employ another doctor at Bratca. There is of course always one doctor in charge but he or she has the hospital, with its twenty eight beds to look after, the clinic in the village to run from eight o'clock in the morning until four o'clock in the afternoon and the orphanage with eighty eight children to oversee, and so there is absolutely no chance for any real involvement with the children. What is needed is one doctor to look after the hospital and clinic and another to care for the children...

Because we don't want another child to die. A forgotten child. That's how we felt about Gyungi. She had been forgotten by her parents, forgotten by staff and forgotten by us. And we all felt terrible when she died.

In 1991 Alex was top dog at Remeti. He was the old-est child in the orphanage, quite bright and could also read and write. The children looked up to him, so the staff used him – and other older boys – to keep control and occasionally he would hit the other children, sometimes, it must be said, with the staff's approval. Some of the younger children were fright-ened of him. In fact he had a gentle heart and was happier in the role of looking after rather than con-trolling the others. He had a confident personality, made friends easily and soon learnt enough English to be able to chat to the volunteers, who soon in their turn learnt a lot about Alex.

They learned that unless it was nailed to the floor it would be stolen, and even if it was nailed down, it, and possibly the nails too, would disappear. Alex was light fingered and it soon became obvious why: he needed the things in order to purchase friendship with people outside in the 'ordinary' world. He would hang around the gate and by the fence talking to the young men of the village, trying to attract their interest. If he could give them a battery, a comb, or a bar of soap, they would say, 'Oh you are a good chap,' or 'What a wonderful fellow you are,' and 'How about trying to get me so and so next time.' So he was always on the lookout for anything he could take which would please them. He had a locker and did keep a very few things for himself, but mainly he gave everything away.

When Alex reached the age of seventeen he seemed destined for Nucet, though it was obviously not the right place for him. Dr Marianna thought the trade school at Oradea would be more suitable. He did not have the necessary entry qualifications, but the authorities turned a blind eye, and Alex was admitted. Many of the students there were streetwise and this suited him. He was to an extent free to go out into Oradea, where he continued his stealing. He has been in prison for a spell but is still at his old game. Still popular, still confident. He is the hero figure, but he is also a thug and probably always will be: perhaps he has no reason not to be.

Viorel was taken into the orphanage when he was very small and simply abandoned there for two years until his mother and grandmother came to fetch him home.

One day, in a drunken rage, his father lashed out with an axe and split Viorel's skull in two places. The village doctor rushed to him and got him into the hospital at Oradea. It was doubtful whether he would survive, but he did. It was felt, however, that there was little chance of him ever returning to normal after such severe head injuries, so he was sent to Cadea. He spent five years fastened to a cot. At the age of nine he was sometimes let out to do small tasks – cleaning and so on – and later was given the job of carrying out the corpses of children who had died in the night.

It was originally believed that children who had suffered such appalling experiences would also suffer nightmares and flashbacks of horror. Astonishingly, it seems that they do not, though some of them do wet their beds. Viorel did until he came to live in England, but from that first night in his new home he never did so again. It may be that a child in Britain (or other stable, prosperous countries) who is badly treated knows he is because he is aware that this is not the norm, but in Romania Viorel and the others never knew anything other than sitting in their cots, experiencing cold, hunger and neglect. In their early years when it was so horrific, the children had little or no language and hardly communicated with each other, though they invented a sort of language of their own. If you sit in a cot day in, day out, with no outside stimulus, how can you think if you have no words? How do you dream? How do you put your feelings into words? Certainly now, with all that in the past, the children seem to be very uncomplicated; they appear cheerful and kind and they bear no visible grudges.

Lorena was born with deformed hands, feet and ankle bones. She has no thumbs, just five fingers on each hand and most probably her feet were similarly deformed. Her records describe her as a bright and sunny child who was quite intelligent. A medical assessment when she was very young decreed that her limbs would never be strong enough to support her body and at the end of her third year her legs were amputated just above the knees. The shock was so great that she regressed rapidly. She looked and behaved like a two-year-old and had to be carried everywhere as she could not walk on the stumps which were the only relics of her legs.

With a great deal of love and help from the volunteers, however, she had the guts to force those stumps into boots, and she learnt to walk and to kick – not only a ball but also the other children! Although only the height of a two-year-old, she was nine or ten by this time, but had still been placed with the younger ones. She was also deaf, having had severe ear infections when very young which had caused both eardrums to burst. A determined survivor despite earlier regression, she had learnt to lip read.

To begin with she was placed with the Salon 6 children, but in 1994, when she was eleven, two ladies from Penryn raised the money for her to come to England for a medical assessment and surgery. To begin with she was given some adequate but rather ugly artificial legs, made of wood and steel. Even so she was completely thrilled with them and particularly with the mirror image of herself, wearing jeans and a smart pullover and looking just like any normal young girl. She would not be parted from those jeans, and when the legs were taken away for some adjustments, she hugged the jeans all day and night.

The artificial legs had been made especially tough, for it was thought that she would be returning to Romania and would have to cope with life at the orphanage. As it turned out, a family wanted to adopt her. After the normal fuss and bother with the social services and courts, Lorena has been allowed to stay. She has a pair of rather more sophisticated legs now, and has also had operations on her ears so that she can hear perfectly well. Her teeth have been straightened so that she is not afraid to smile. She has grown her hair long, she goes to school, speaks fluent English and appears to be a happy, sociable girl with a great sense of humour. She keeps in touch with Pat and if one of Pat's dogs knocks her down in a fit of exuberance, she just laughs, picks herself up and gets ready if necessary to be knocked down again if the dogs are especially friendly.

Ramona is a little blonde-haired girl who was seven years old when the first volunteers saw her. She was in her cot, unable to sit up or speak. Everyone thought she was mentally retarded and she was known affectionately as 'The Blob'. Then her sponsor in England wrote and illustrated a story called 'Princess Ramona'. One by one the volunteers would take Ramona out of her cot, sit her on their laps, read the story to her and show her the pictures. Something – the story, the pictures, the pleasure of sitting on someone's lap, the special attention – triggered an interest in her. Suddenly she began to respond; she began to sit up, to talk and to walk. At first her talking was gobbledegook, but now she speaks normally. Although she needs more specialist care, she is a happy, smiling child, quite content to live in an institution.

Not every sponsor makes such an imaginative gift as the story which changed Ramona's life, but each sponsor does make a difference to the child or children they help support. As well as the money they contribute (£100 a year), a real link is established between the sponsors and the children. Most children in the orphanages know the word 'sponsor' and what it means. Hopefully it creates a little warm feeling that someone far away cares for them. Sponsors can and do send cards, gifts and photographs to 'their' children and they receive regular reports on their progress, based mainly on observations brought back by returning volunteers.

The sponsorship scheme, which started in 1992, is organized by the secretary, Kay Toms. There are 98 sponsors to date, some of whom sponsor more than one child, but at least 40 more are needed at the time of writing. Some children are sponsored by volunteers who have worked with them and then returned to Britain, some sponsors have come forward after talks given by volunteers or White Cross workers, others have been attracted to the scheme through the

White Cross shop in Truro or have called Kay for more information. On occasion a school has contacted Kay to say that a class would like to sponsor a child of their own age, and families have done the same. Some people ask specifically to support a handicapped child, others ask for a child who is able to write back to them.

Kay really seems to 'see' the children, if not always in the flesh, but from what she knows of them through the illuminating records sent her by the volunteers. Kay and Sue Pearce, the White Cross secretary, visited Romania for a fortnight in 1993 and Kay gives delightful glimpses of the children she met on her visit in a little unpublished booklet called *The Romanian Experience*.

> We heard a few children along a corridor, running, and I came face to face with Erika. I recognised her immediately. It was strange, seeing this face I knew so well, that I had looked at so many times in her file, back home on my desk. Suddenly, I felt, in a funny way, relaxed. Everything was so strange and new, we had come such a long way, but here was a familiar face. It must have been confusing for Erika, to be hugged by a strange lady. However, she didn't seem too surprised. These children who had had no one for so very long are only too happy to hug everyone. Erika is quite a mature,

undemanding young lady, and she had not pre-pared me for the hunger and fervour of some of her friends. I had known the phrase, 'being loved to death', but in Remeti I found out what it meant…

It's amazing how easy it is to communicate with these children. They know some English, and have worked out a way of communicating with the volunteers. Viorel and I talked about his beloved 'Mama Pat' back in England. I had lots of hugs from Viorel on the strength of my friendship with Mama Pat (for the first time I could really appreciate the saying, 'it's not what you know, but whom you know')…

Next in line are the older girls, and I suppose the leader, by sheer pushiness is Elena. Elena has a beautiful, open, freckled face, but there's an uncertainty about her. She has very wide-open eyes, but never quite smiles, or relaxes. She strangles when she hugs, pushes others away to sit beside you, commands and demands your attention and then stares straight into your face with her unreadable, unblinking eyes. Clara is a very thin, ordinary looking girl – until she smiles. Then her eyes disappear, and her face lights up. Clara just radiates happiness. She too is undemanding, content to sit beside you, beam-ing, when she's not dancing…

The younger children jump on you, kiss you, hug you. Bujorel, quite strong, almost pulling me over once or twice, gazing into my face, staring at my hands, and gently examining each finger. He was looking at my nails, and then I noticed that most of the children had nails bitten down to the quick...

And Stefan, who came to Remeti a few weeks ago. He was found on the bridge at Oradea, beaten, dirty, neglected. There isn't an inch of his body that is not scarred, and the wounds on his head and face were still too painful for us to touch. Stefan was at the beginning of his life with us, a frightened, abused, traumatized child. I watched him in the Relaxation Room, an experience I will never forget. He curled up on the mat, listening intently to the music, a look of pain on his poor little damaged face. He beckoned to me to lie down beside him, then he held my head next to his head. There was such a terrible look of despair on his face, I felt he would cry, but there were no tears. If it is possible to cry silently, Stefan was crying loud enough to fill that building. The tension and pain in that room became so unbearable that we had to switch the music off. Stefan slowly uncurled, got up, and appeared to have come back from some dark, dreadful, hellish place...

During their visit, Kay and Sue had the chance to accompany some of the children to a Romanian Orthodox church service. The children receive no religious education at school, but those who are able to behave appropriately and make something of the services do attend the local church regularly. They love dressing up smartly for church and seem to enjoy the experience even though the Orthodox service is so lengthy. The colour, drama, chanting, incense, the sense of occasion and the gorgeous robes of the priests are all fascinating to them. Some of the children can recite parts of the service by heart, but it is difficult to tell how much they understand, although they undoubtedly gain some feeling of God from the awe and mystery conveyed by the service. As Pat says, 'Something must rub off on them.' Kay describes the whole experience vividly:

I was very keen to go to church, and so was Sue. Peter said if we two and Vicky would go with him we could manage a large group of children. The service actually began at eight o'clock continuing till lunch time. Peter said we would leave at about eleven o'clock, this leaving the right amount of time to ensure interest and good behaviour from the children. It was a long time until eleven o'clock, a beautiful day, so I decided to wander over to the Spital to talk to any child I could find. I found a little group playing around the swings. It's strange how easy it is to talk to children without knowing their language. They make it so easy, with actions, face pulling, mimes, mixtures of foreign words they know. And being a Latin based language, many of the words are familiar. It was easy to understand Violeta when she asked if we were going to the 'Basilica'. Violeta was able to tell me who would not be going. The list of those allowed to go was as follows: Violeta, Tomi, Ana, Ramona, Nicolina, Emil, Maria, Robert, Attila, Szabolcs, Leidi, Gusti and Pinti. Immediately, Elemer was at my elbow, with a pathetic face, stubbing a finger in his chest and pleading, 'Elemer Basilica! Elemer Basilica'!

Why not Elemer? I asked Violeta. He seemed a very sweet, well behaved boy.

'No Elemer!' Violeta said with a fierce face. 'Elemer – Basilica – Waa! Waa! Waa!'

The others joined in with impressions of Elemer screaming, crying, stamping his feet. I turned to Elemer, who was standing very quietly beside me.

'Is this true Elemer?' I asked. 'Basilica – you – Waa! Waa! Waa?' Elemer sadly nodded his head...

At ten o'clock Peter came over from the apartment with the boxes of 'church clothes'. Jeans and T-shirts were taken off, and the boys put on the smartest shirts and trousers, and the girls pretty dresses. They all looked so wonderful. We walked to church arriving about eleven thirty. 'The only thing you need to know,' Peter told me at the church door, 'is that women sit on one side, and the men on the other.'

We entered the church. It appeared to be square in shape, with the priest and altar to the right, men and boys sitting in rows around him, and to the left in rows sat the women and girls and young children. There was a middle section in front of us, where bored children or maybe children who hadn't decided yet which sex they were, wandered between male and female relatives. The walls were covered with huge paintings and drapes, there were hundreds of candles, and in the area where the priest and his helpers stood, chandeliers glittered with candles. Surrounding the priest were numerous huge, round loaves, all with tall candles stuck in their middles.

And the floor to ceiling was heavy with incense and the deep, sad singing of women, so much part of the building that you felt them and breathed them in as you walked inside.

The hazy, humming, perfumed church was full. Peter took the older boys to a free space with the men, and they stayed there for the rest of the service. It was interesting to see how serious and involved the boys were. It was as if they had been coming to this service every Sunday for the whole of their lives. They knew when to cross themselves, when to join in, they listened intently to the priest when he gave his long (long!) sermon. I thought as I watched them how steeped they are in the customs, faith and rituals of their own country, and how good it would be to find them homes in their own land...

I couldn't see a spare space amongst the women, so I sat down on the steps between the rows. Leidi stayed close beside me all the time. Ana and Ramona talked to all the babies and toddlers, sitting by various smiling mothers. Ramona was eventually adopted by a group of teenage girls, who sat her beside them, and kept smiling at her and giving her flowers. Many of the younger children held small posies of flowers.

Violeta sat by me some of the time, some of the time by Sue, and a lot of the time she marched around supervising the younger ones.

Tomi and Attila sat for a while with Peter, then came to sit by us. Tomi was quite involved in the service. Attila ended up sitting by some older ladies, picture-book peasants with lined brown faces, head scarves and drab dark jumpers and skirts. He had a long involved conversation with these ladies – I wonder what he told them about me, he waved his hands in my direction at one time and the ladies nodded and gave me happy smiles.

It was wonderful! The music and the incense swelling around us, the strange faces, some of them stern, many of them eventually smiling. The chanting, sonorous music, strange, unknown words, that went on and on. Then, suddenly, the music in my head was clearer, louder, and I realised I was humming! I knew this tune!

O Lord my God! When I in awesome wonder...

I was humming loudly, happily. Leidi looked at me in surprise. 'I know this tune!' I told her. 'England, this tune!' Leidi understood (of course) and smiled.

O Lord my God! When I in awesome wonder
Consider all the works Thy hand hath made
I see the stars, I hear the mighty thunder
Thy power throughout the universe displayed.

Then sings my soul, my Saviour God to Thee:
    How great Thou art! How great Thou art!
Then sings my soul, my Saviour God to Thee:
    How great Thou art! How great Thou art!

As Kay and Sue sang this hymn that day in the 'Basilica', it reminded them how faith in the power of

God was so much at the heart of all that the White Cross Mission was doing. After all, it was Pat's faith and that of those who supported her that had brought it all into being. Without it, these children would not be there in church drinking in the atmosphere. Pat, the driving force behind the White Cross, possesses an unshakeable belief that God, although transcending humankind absolutely, calls and needs people to cooperate with Him, to exert heart, mind, soul and strength in love and compassion when others are in desperate need. This, of course, is what the White Cross Mission is all about and Pat has always had a faith which, rooted in Jesus, has humanity at its heart.

In 1992, the year after the White Cross Mission was born, Pat was made minister in charge of St Enoder Parish, Cornwall, and in June 1994 was one of the first women priests to be ordained by the Church of England. Some may be critical of the idea that anyone could be involved in two such major undertakings – being at the heart of the White Cross Mission and being in charge of a parish. Surely either the parishioners or the children lose out? In fact she fulfils her pastoral and other duties perfectly. The congregation has increased since she arrived and she has rescued the parish from debt and neglect. She is not ambitious for herself, she wants only to use what gifts she has to serve.

Pat visits Romania at regular intervals, for ten days or so every two or three months. The focus is always on the children and it is essential for the Mission's leaders to plan ahead carefully in order to ensure a positive future for the children and to develop the care that is available for them.

In February 1994 Pat, accompanied by Jahal de Meritens and Jeff Saville, went to Bucharest with the specific purpose of doing what they could to plan the long-term future of the children. They paid a flying visit to Bratca and Remeti to see how the children and the volunteers were getting on, then they had an important meeting with officials and others who could be involved in plans for the future. They met with the British Ambassador, the Anglican priest-in-charge in Bucharest, the local manager of *Pentru Copii Nostri* (Romanian Orphanage Trust), two newspaper editors, a representative of the Ministry of Health, the Assistant Director of Health in Oradea, and the White Cross Mission lawyer.

It was made clear that the Romanian authorities were unwilling to make any change to their original diagnosis of all the children as 'irrecuperable', which means that they are regarded as committed mental patients destined for transference to an adult psychiatric unit when they reach the age of eighteen. After much discussion they did relent to the extent of being willing to consider the provision of workshops to keep the children occupied within the system.

Pat wrote, 'We are totally committed to changing the system and have been plotting and scheming to bring about a new way of thinking … we can tell you that the Romanian journalists and the Orthodox and Anglican churches are following our progress with interest.'

On returning to the UK and reporting to the other directors, a decision was made to raise the money to purchase a house so that the White Cross had a permanent home to offer some of the children. One important step forward in this respect was to be the founding of a sister charity known as *Foundation Crucea Alba*, with a committee consisting of two members of the White Cross Mission and five Romanians. They would be responsible for surveying and purchasing farms or houses, employing house-parents and supervising the running of the houses as village homes for some of the children as soon as the authorities deemed them suitable for release to such a way of life. Pat was confident that this agreement would be secured in the end.

Running such houses was one way in which the children's normality might be secured. Another way was to encourage Romanian families to foster the children and hundreds of letters were given to several priests to hand round to the villagers.

In October 1994 the Suffragan Bishop of Truro went out with Pat to visit the children at Remeti and Bratca. While there the Bishop and Pat, by now ordained as a priest, officiated in an Orthodox church service, which lasted for four hours, for most of which time they had to stand fully robed. Pat later told how 'Bishop Graham was busy taking note of all the customs and traditions and was particularly impressed when two little ladies knelt at the priest's feet during his reading of the Gospel and ducking down under his robes began kissing his feet. Bishop Graham thought this custom could well be introduced into the Diocese of Truro!'

At the end of the Bishop's visit the White Cross Mission held a special reception in Bucharest for the British Ambassador, Bishop Teofan, several other dignitaries, and television, radio and newspaper reporters. The aim was to celebrate the work which had already been done at Remeti and Bratca and to publicize the ongoing needs. Display boards at the reception told the story of the White Cross Mission.

The highlight of the occasion came when seven of the children from Remeti appeared. Viorel solemnly went up to the Ambassador, shook him by the hand and said in his best Oxford accent, 'Hello. Do you speak English?' The children were beautifully dressed in national costumes made by people in Cornwall; they sang four songs, accompanied by Horia on a portable electric piano.

While the main purpose of the event was to make clear the fact that these children are normal and healthy and should not be locked away or branded as 'irrecuperables', it proved to be an epic and thrillingly memorable event for the children themselves.

The excitement of the occasion from the point of view of the children is beautifully described in an account of the trip called 'Is this Bucuresti?', written by Torrie Perryman who was one of the volunteers involved.

'Time for choir practice' are the words that stick in my mind upon my arrival at the Woodhouse – A choir? – not only a choir, but music provided by Horia, who only five days previously had requested to try the electric organ. He played all four songs near perfect after only ever having heard them once before. Sebastien was redundant.

During preparations by the volunteers for the concert, Dr Marianna, Maria and Sanda worked tirelessly – listening to the practices, playing conductor and altering, washing and pressing clothes and costumes for the two-day trip. Without their help we would surely never have been able to co-ordinate or choreograph what ended up as a fabulous event. How fantastic to see the results of Romanians and English working as a united team. Well Done Everyone.

A lift in a prehistoric ambulance takes us from Remeti to the station in Ciucea. Is this Bucuresti? The train drew into the station and we scrambled through the darkness across the tracks loading luggage, food and children onto a train that stopped barely three minutes – find the sleeping compartments – settle – trips to the toilet and bed. 8 a.m. – Bucuresti. 'Is this Bucuresti?' We settle in the station restaurant, all tired from the ten-hour journey. Trips to the toilet, Fanta and coffee all round. The metro, Horia's train noises are hauntingly real. 'Is this Bucuresti?' As we leave the tube we count all the children.

Burgers, Ketchup, Mustard and Fries – eyes full of wonder, stomachs full of food. Is this Bucuresti? We walked to the cultural centre, Graham in the middle of the road playing Lollipop man. Not a stocking in sight, Oh Boy! can that man stop traffic.

We arrive – we change. Seven orphans transformed by national costume into proud citizens. Mingling at ease with diplomats, church fathers and the press. Elena eyes up the Bishop of Romania's beard with great interest – we all think 'Oh no Elena'; somehow she manages to realise this is not the time to pull it, lick it or blow on it. We sit, Pat speaks, the kids sit still. It's time. Their special moment has arrived after weeks of preparation. They sing – seven children written off by society, sing their hearts out, not knowing who to or what for.

I cried, as did many other, inwardly or outwardly. Applause, smiles – Is this Bucuresti?

Goodbyes and tears, laughter and thanks to the children for their beautiful concert.

As we left Bucuresti the children got quieter and quieter as the exhaustion of the day and the impact of the event began to sink in. Each of them taking away different parts of a special day in their memories and hearts for ever. The station. 'Is this Bucuresti?' The train – find the carriage, food and Fanta quick. This time no beds, but pull-out seats on which to huddle and keep warm. We all drift off to sleep with strains of 'Un Elefant' seeping into our dreams. 5 a.m. 'Is this Bucuresti?' The train stops. Into a freezing Romanian morning, the train goes on, we huddle in tired silence in the ambulance and all too soon arrive back at the Spital; a child wakes up sleepily. 'Is this Bucuresti?' No, that was Bucuresti.

Thank you: Elena, Viorel, Gusti, Horia, Erika, Rita and Clara – with all our hearts. (Naomi, Sue, Darren, Sebastien, Torrie, Tig and Graham – volunteers)

7

The escape route

The concert was a memorable day for all, boosted by a sense of occasion. Yet, although a very special one, the trip was typical of that made by any group of children, full of boisterous good spirits, enjoying an outing and suddenly free from ordinary routine and surroundings. Horia and the other children revelled in the rare excitement of a train journey. But they were always on another train going one way – its destination Nucet, the adult mental institution where, under the present scheme of things, every one of the children was destined to spend the rest of his or her life. One child had already been sent there and had run away. He did not like the beatings and the injections. What hope is there for the rest?

Since they are still labelled as 'irrecuperables', and the authorities seem reluctant to change the ruling that all such cases are sent to adult institutions at the age of eighteen, time is running out for many of the older children. Every escape route for them has to be explored to the full. One continuing hope has been that some children will be offered foster homes by kindly Romanian families. In 1994 Pat took two hundred letters translated by Dr Morgenstern at St Columb Minor to Popa Gheorge, a priest at Doloreni, Popa Liviu at Bratca and Popa Marius at Remeti. They all agreed to distribute the letters, which contained details on how to go about fostering children. 'If we find just one family it will be worth the trouble,' Pat said. Also a few children have been or are in the process of being adopted by families in other countries.

The other solution, and perhaps the best when it works out successfully, has now been approved by the authorities. Gradually properties are being bought: houses or farms where a group of children with a degree of self-reliance can live together as a family in the care of a housemother and foster parents. The process is still very much in the early stages, but one house is up and running, with more being prepared.

All the foster parents will be employed on a ten-year contract, which means that all the children can reach the age of twenty-one before being left to manage on their own, at which point the houses will become the property of the children themselves. Until then they will be owned jointly by the White Cross Mission and *Foundation Crucea Alba*. The housemothers will be paid a salary equivalent to that of one of the spital nurses – £500 per annum – and hopefully the sponsors will continue to contribute

towards the care of the individual children. The foster
fathers will be encouraged to continue with their own
jobs and the children taught how to work the land
and to become self-supporting. In addition it is hoped
that a parish or firm back in the UK might be willing
to sponsor each family and farm and that this money,
added to the local Romanian family allowance, will
help each family group over the most difficult first
few years.

Early in 1995 Pat walked round the village of
Bratca with some of the volunteers and Popa Liviu,
looking for properties for sale. They saw seven, rang-
ing in price from £500 to £8,000. One was particularly
charming. Set on the side of a mountain and with
grape vines clustering round the veranda, it offered a
beautiful vista of fields sloping down to the river.
Another had acres of plum trees and was in an even
more idyllic position. But they had to be sensible.
Price might be a more important factor than the view.

Buying a house is often fraught with snags and in
Romania it is no different. They went out one day to
clinch a deal and found that the property had been
sold the day before. Another time they arrived to find
that the price was not what they had expected. At
times, however, the unexpected played into their
hands. Lynn, one of the volunteers, wrote:

As luck would have it the Mayor had just heard
of another property and there was the wife just

passing the window, so we went out instantly, we saw it, loved it and bought it. It all happened rather fast, not at all like you would expect in Romania. [Apparently one affinity between Romania and Cornwall is the 'do it d'reckly' mentality.] The deal was concluded at midnight with us all counting out our dollars on the owner's best table with the Mayor, the Priest, Pat, Philip, Graham, Judy and myself, the owner and his wife. We managed to make a sketch plan of the house and farm and inspect the well. There seems to be a buffalo wagon in the barn. The Mayor gave Judy her first lesson in scything, as it is important to keep the grass cut. The house is really Romanian with red tiles, unrendered brick and with limed, traditionally stencilled walls and ceiling.

This first house, 'Casa Fericita' (House of Happiness), had first to be kitted out with electrics, plumbing and fittings; then in September 1996 six children from Remeti – Bela, Andrei, Claudia, Mandinita, Macoy and Attila – left the spital for their new home. Much to everyone's relief, the Health Department and the Social Services agreed to the transference of the children after they had been formally identified, their parents found and all the legal work completed.

Now as I write in 1997 'Casa Fericita' is continuing to be a great success. Claudine, a 'housemum', Florica and Nelu and Livia the foster parents are all coping admirably. Nelu brought his six sheep up to the house over the winter and they had lambs during January. Recently he brought eight sheep for the children to keep. Six of these have had lambs too so they are already embarking on a small business which, it is hoped, will eventually bring some money into the family.

Andrei, aged sixteen, is in charge of the sheep and all the other children have their own special jobs. Attila is in charge of both chopping wood and feeding the fires with it; Bela takes Florica's little girl to school, meets her afterwards and when he is in the village he also does the daily shopping. He is going to be in charge of the vegetable garden once they get it started. Macoy does the hoovering and looks after Bobby the dog, and Claudia does the washing up. They all take their turns at cooking and are pretty expert at making delicious doughnuts. (Mandinita had to return to the hospital, sadly, but it is possible that another child will go in her place.) The house is warm and clean and everything is working so well. Jill and Roger Hamer visited it for a few weeks at Christmas in 1996 and gave a glowing account of its warm and friendly atmosphere. They also talked of a neighbouring Romanian family who are now firm friends.

'Trandafir' (Romanian for rose) is the second house and is so called because the Roseland Friends Group raised the money to buy it. This is the 'honey pot' house. Seven and a half acres of fruit trees mean that this house should be self-sufficient immediately after the first fruit harvest, and once a still is installed it should double the income. The potential is considerable, but the trees have been neglected for years and need pruning and tending and the house itself is in a poor state. There is a lot to do there, but it is just about to be attacked by the miracle-working maintenance men, so in time all will be well. When 'Trandafir' is ready, another six children will take up their residence there.

The most likely third house to be bought is one in Remeti, on the road to the mountains. During 1995 and 1996 eleven students from Truro School, guided by teacher Jenny Leathes, raised £8,000 to buy a house. The project was part of the Duke of Edinburgh Award Scheme and they presented the cheque to Pat in December 1996. Twenty-four hours later Anoushka Turner, one of the students, was rushed to hospital with meningitis. Before long, she died. The house, purchased with the £8,000, will be called 'Anoushka's House' in her memory. Next year several of the other students are planning to go to Romania with Jenny to see the house and do some voluntary work. The house is a good size, in excellent condition with a spring of water and a bathroom already in place. The land that accompanies the house is flat and fertile, stretching down to the river. It is hoped that with a couple of polytunnels, provided by the Young Farmers of Cornwall, the children could be the first in the market each year with produce.

The whole project of placing some of the children in homes within the wider community is in one sense experimental, inevitably. But it is legally secure and has the backing and support of both the Romanian authorities and the Anglican and Orthodox churches. It is also expensive! Supporters of the White Cross Mission are already experienced in the art of giving and it seems they will need to do more.

It is not only money which is needed, however. The giving of time and expertise is just as vital for the continuing survival and gradual recovery of the 'irrecuperables'. Many individuals and groups have given so generously over the years so far. They have achieved so much in their own way for the children at Remeti and Bratca, and it is to be hoped that such priceless support will continue now that the work is moving into new areas and the children's needs change.

Some people have stayed only for a few days, but the professional help and advice they have given is invaluable. One such is Dr Amir, a dentist to the rich and famous, including Jon Bon Jovi and Frank Bruno. He offered to go to Romania and in April 1996 there he was, working hard. For the three days of his visit he started work at 7 a.m. examining the teeth all the one hundred and sixty seven children at

Remeti and Bratca. He pulled teeth, filled others, and began comprehensive records not only for the children but also for the villagers, who were delighted. Many of them had had no access to a dentist for years, and had suffered the poison and pain of rotting teeth. One young girl had all her front teeth pulled out, and one might have imagined that she would be devastated, but she was delighted. For the first time since she could remember, she was free from pain. It is possible too, that some of the 'peculiar' behaviour of the children, such as repeated headbanging, could be a reaction to the misery of pain. Dr Amir has been back to Romania twice since that first trip and hopes to continue making regular visits to the children.

Cheryl Berriman, a Speech and Language Therapist who works for the Health Department in Cornwall, went out in 1995 with Harriet Nott, who works for the County Audiology Service. Cheryl went out again in 1996, to train the Romanian 'educators', mainly in Bratca. She had the help of Maria and one or two other translators. While there she was invited to give some lectures to Romanian specialists and is grateful for what she also learnt from them. Cheryl tells the story of her first visit in her own words:

> I am a speech and language therapist working in a special school for children with severe learning difficulties and children with special needs in mainstream school. Pat got a group of us

together and said, 'They don't talk properly, we want you to help us, is there anything we can do?'

'But we don't speak Romanian.'

'What exactly do you mean "talk properly"?'

(Hungarian, Romanian, Gypsy, English – HELP)

'What are the children like?'

'What do you want – ideas, equipment? How can an English speech therapist help?'

'I'd love to see Romania.'

'You'd better go and have a look,' said Pat.

I wanted to take an audiometer to test their hearing (are they deaf?). 'I'll come with you,' said Harriet, our teacher of the deaf. So on Easter Monday the two of us, two audiometers, other electrical bits, about half a ton of batteries, a ream of paper, card, pens, information and a change of clothes, set off to Bratca and Remeti.

First to Remeti, what do we do? Well, Patrika now has a communication folder, so that he can make choices about what he will do, and tell volunteers about what he has done before. Robbi is now the proud owner of a hearing aid. Lots of advice and ideas. We sat on the veranda writing notes, programmes, and making up picture and story books. Maria joined in as a translator, so now Remeti has a stock of books in Romanian to use with the children.

Memories of Remeti are mixed with an Orthodox Easter – sleepy girls from the Spital in church, at midnight, hundreds of people outside holding candles, children everywhere wanting their share of 1,500 chocolate Creme Eggs. A few hours sneaked away to climb a mountain, and have a coffee and cake with a Romanian family, and then sadly we bid farewell as we left for Bratca.

We had many positive feelings about Bratca. The rooms, now painted with murals, are the best I have ever worked in. More work with Harriet as we started hearing tests, slowly working out who has a hearing loss, and who had poor listening skills, what was wrong with the talking, what English volunteers might do. Then it was back to writing reports and making up packages or 'work packages' ready for the next group of volunteers to use.

This time, it's rain, shops and the sound of trains going through as we worked that will remind me of Bratca. Soon the two weeks were over.

We'd both love to come back, but jobs and family rule out a long stay. Was it worth it? From our side most definitely. We're heading home with lists of things to do in Britain. Thank you especially to Graham, for all the time and effort that he put into our stay, to

Hannah for her help at Bratca which we couldn't have managed without and to Maria for all her translating, but especially thank you to the children who were so welcoming and tolerant to these people who 'beeped' machines at them, demanded that they perform tasks, say words, and try to sign. They were wonderful and enthusiastic (on the whole).

As we leave, clutching our now well thumbed copy of *Colloquial Romanian*, I suspect we leave behind memories of those two who 'Don't Talk Properly…'

Harriet, too, wrote an account of her visit:

I was told Robbi had a hearing problem but I expected to find many more … by rights they should all have hearing problems, their conditions being less than ideal.

In a Cornish 'special' school for the best part of a year a substantial number of children would be inflicted with the 'glue ear' type problems, you know the symptoms, continuous thick catarrh, that bunged up, blocked up feeling…

Remeti … the mountains, and not a grotty nose in sight. A lot of the children not only had normal hearing – but positively 'sharp' hearing.

Thinking about the reasons for this I considered,

1) Was it that the air was better at Remeti; the dampness of the Cornish mists are renowned for causing wheezes and rheumatism?

2) Healthwise, do the children in fact benefit from being in conditions that aren't over warm and protective?

Or is it that these are the fittest of the surviving children?

I don't know – maybe it was just a good day. But it was pleasing to know that a lot of the children at Remeti are most definitely 'tuned in'. I'm not sure what they thought of the woman creeping up behind them and scrunching, rattling, bleeping and burping but they did enjoy my warbles. Robbi tried out his hearing aid and seemed well pleased – at least I think that's why he kissed it. Typically adolescent, the thing that he enjoyed mostly was the sound of his own voice, as he sang into his microphone grinning. He has a long way to go yet with regards to his hearing/listening, but he seems to have developed his own strategies for survival. He's becoming well known and liked within the community of Remeti. He's a confident communicator and learnt that helping people with their bags of shopping/wood, earns friendship, thanks, oh and the odd 'suc' (soft drink).

Moving on to Bratca and the grotty noses – the wheezy chests – the runny ears, and yes –

the hearing problems. One out of the ten tests had normal, sharp hearing but it didn't need much explaining, the smoky Spital, the children's lack of mobility and sunshine. Hopefully the summer will help ... and maybe I can come back with something more positive, like a few hearing aids to help the younger more able children with their language.

I was told I'd be surviving on turnips here ... (by a doctor) ... I've been well fed, supported and looked after by everybody, especially Graham. (I'll just have to start the diet when I get home now.) It's been great to work alongside Cheryl, the speech therapist. I thought I knew a lot, but coming here I realised I know so little.

Another special visit was from the Rotaract group. Rotaract is a worldwide organization of young people aged from 18 to 29 which undertakes community and international service projects. Founded in 1968 by Rotary International, its motto is 'Friendship in action'. A team of Rotaractors had offered to lend a hand to the White Cross and Hannah's *Gazette* article 'Could This Be Them' best describes the impact they made.

Chris and myself were busying around the apartment trying to solve the problem of where the hell we were going to sleep nineteen people from the Rotaract Group, due to arrive that day.

We decided that five could sleep at Graham's, five could sleep in the apartment and the remaining ones 'God only knows' – well little did we know but God was just around the corner. I don't believe this is written in the Bible, but it turns out he's changed his name to Tudor and he's now the Mayor of Bratca. Tudor offered us two rooms above his offices to put up the others. It was hardly 'Breakfast at Tiffany's', but they were warm, dry and comfortable and it was very much appreciated.

Graham arrived later that day and we all waited in anticipation of their arrival. The slightest sound of a vehicle coming within one hundred yards of the apartment made us leap from our seats and shout 'Could this be them?' The following evening I accompanied my surrogate mother and father to the bar where we had the usual double measure of vodka and coke for 30p, eyes constantly glued to the window. After the bar Graham went off to his house and Chris and I headed to the apartment. Chris went off to bed, but as usual I couldn't get to sleep so I lit the customary candle and rolled a cigarette with the sweet smelling Golden Virginia tobacco *mama* and *tata* had sent out for me.

THEN SUDDENLY … The crowd roared, three English minibuses were heading down the road – it was 12.30 a.m.

After throwing on some clothes I gave Chris a yell and we both went down to meet the onslaught. Having got the introductions out of the way we all went to the bar – THE BAR ...? Yes the bar; it was now approximately 1.15 a.m. Graham met us in the bar and when we'd all sufficiently wetted our palates we all went off to our various abodes for the night.

Neither Graham or myself bothered going to bed, instead we talked about the plans for the Rotaract Group and the do's and don'ts newcomers need to consider when living in Romania. This all took place in the kitchen alongside various catering packets of tuna, marmalade, biscuits and spam.

The following day work began for all, I was doing my usual impression of a headless chicken trying to organise things and find a storeroom for the materials the group had brought. Well it was all change for God Tudor, Mayor of Bratca, because as if by magic he had now turned into MR BEN and was making things happen swiftly and simply. Yes you've guessed it – MR BEN had a store-room, WHAT A HERO...

Various meetings were held with Domnul Doctor to look over the plans of the Spital, the group then got on with the jobs required. They all showed great enthusiasm and seemed to thrive on the fact that they only had a short time in which to complete their tasks. The four activity rooms we now have in the main Spital were totally transformed. In the children's Spital, the group were knocking down walls and plastering up door-ways in the laundry rooms to make several rooms for each process, washing, drying and ironing clothes, etc.

They worked alongside Romanians and each day for brunch were subjected to *palinka*, sausage, bread and gerkins … mmm … nice … Odd jobs around the Spital were done, repairing the electricity, doors and windows, with plenty of help of course.

During their stay the apartment was complete chaos, with rucksacks, clothes, food and cooking equipment everywhere – but it was the most welcome chaos Bratca has ever seen and we are eternally grateful. I can also speak for all the children, who for those of you who don't know have had no activity rooms before, making it difficult and frustrating for both volunteers and children alike – but thanks to Rotaract we can now enjoy and benefit from their hard work.

Brian Stoyel, the leader of the Rotaract Group, tells the story from their perspective:

Working with the White Cross Mission in Bratca, the Rotaractors spent two weeks repairing doors and windows, fixing and installing new lighting, and demolishing, building, and painting walls. In addition to this essential repair work, the crew of amateur carpenters created three new rooms, complete with colourful murals, which will be used by children for learning and play activities. Filling the room are frisbees, footballs, and an array of other toys and educational materials that the Rotaractors had brought with them, along with some urgently needed medical supplies.

In many respects, getting their minibus and two vans with their load of humanitarian aid to Bratca was the most challenging part of the project. The group spent five and a half hours in freezing weather at the Austria/Hungary border while every item they were carrying was checked and translated into Hungarian. What could have been even worse delays were averted at the Romanian border thanks to a friendly Romanian who spent three hours helping us unravel documentation irregularities.

But the hardship and hard work were quickly eclipsed by the children's happiness. Wearing donated teddy bear T-shirts, the children responded with joy and laughter when they saw their new rooms with the toys and bright murals – a sight our Rotaractors found far more heart-warming than any tropical sun would have been.

One of this Rotaract Group, Rob Wilde, just had to come back!

I had been to Bratca at Easter '95 with the Rotaract refurbishing/painting team. It won my heart and as soon as I came home I began to look forward to my next visit. October 1995 had been my hoped for travel date, but there were one or two cats thrown into the pigeons. At one stage, after problems with my MSc studies and a completely flooded flat due to burst pipes, I thought I was doomed not to return. However, determined to reach Bratca, on 15th January I headed for Heathrow and a flight to Bucharest.

I was a little nervous about the journey as I knew I was going to travel with Graham, who I knew, and PAT ROBSON – THE DIRECTOR OF THE WHITE CROSS and a LADY OF THE CLOTH! What would it be like – I'd imagined quiet and boring (I'd never met Pat before!). I needn't have worried, we all had quite a laugh on our trek across Europe – Fab!! It was also great to be with Viorel, Pat's son from Remeti, as he experienced his first return to Romania.

The overnight train journey to Oradea was fun – we had a picnic and Graham was overcome as I produced some iced Christmas cake! After our supper we all lurched off to our beds. Pat shared her bed with a famous author, Graham shared his with Elkie Brookes and I shared mine with various artists (on our Walkmans). The line from Bucharest to Oradea is quite a bumpy one – either that or CFR trains have square wheels. Are you supposed to get sea-sick on a train?

We arrived in a rather cold Bratca at 9.30 a.m. on Tuesday morning, to be met by a greeting party of Hannah, Philip and Rebecca – it was just like 'Brief Encounter'. After a much needed cuppa, a general natter and unloading of my excess luggage, I was raring to go – the Romanian bit of my character was back! 'Let me at the Spital.'

Since I had been before there were now another thirty kids in the Spital from Nucet. It was quite noticeable the negative effect that this had had on some of the original Bratca children. However, I am comforted by the fact that the White Cross programme will reverse this negative trend and that things will now be on the up again.

It was excellent to see all of the children that I knew again. I had wondered how many would remember me – they must see so many faces. Surprisingly, and quite touchingly, many remembered me – it was lovely. A particularly 'memorable' moment for me was when Ionel, the young man who I sponsor, first saw me – he ran over to me, threw himself at me and gave me a big hug. At this point I got some dust in my eye and it began to water … OK, so it made me cry.

I could talk about the children for ages – it is impossible not to love each and every one of them. Young Jenika had made so much progress since I last saw her – walking, dancing and the most gorgeous laugh and smile ever – what a cutie. I don't know if Camelia, the little epileptic girl could remember me – she is so dazed, but as ever, she sat there chuckling and laughing most infectiously, happily playing with her piece of string. I won't give a description of each child, let's just say they are all fab, ace and lovely and very special…

Away from the Spital, Bratca life was, as ever, an experience! The local entertainment came from an evening in the Non-Stop bar – quite a cabaret. There are not many places where you can see a boxing match unofficially (OK it was a brawl), a rather odd but totally addictive Romanian pop video starring a plucked chicken and a potential pork chop…

Romania continues to amaze me, it is an excellent country and I feel very much at home there. Not just Bratca, although that is where my 'love affair' began, but the whole country. I spent my last few days with a friend in Oradea where I saw a totally different Romania, but equally as appealing.

My stay in the country ended on a high. As the Oradea-Bucharest train ripped through a rather cold Bratca, I stuck my head out of the window and waved at Graham, Juliet, Rebecca and Nelu who stood huddled on the station; -20ºC + 60mph = FROSTBITE, but I was determined to say my last goodbye.

'*Ciao* Bratca. I'll be back' – and I mean it, I will be back. Just try to keep me away!

Two community nurses and a community resource worker give their reactions to the time they spent with the children:

We arrived in Romania on Tuesday 29th August, after three and a half days travelling in a wheelie bin disguised as a minibus.

Wednesday 30th, and three of us descended on Bratca hospital. Myself – Emma a community nurse (RNMH) – Hayley my colleague also a community nurse (RNMH) and Stewart a community resource worker at a day service.

Within twenty minutes we managed to disrupt the hospital causing chaos in our wake. Nothing could have prepared us for our reception; each of our limbs held at least two children vying for our attention. It is difficult to describe our feelings – so many emotions.

Only seven working days later, we are due to leave. Our main purpose to experience some of the needs of the hospital and the children, hopefully achieved in order to raise funds and sponsors for people who could return for a longer period of time with many different skills.

We feel we have given very little to the children, but we have gained so much. Each of us fell in love with individual children for different reasons; for their strengths, needs, cheekiness, naughtiness, smiles and hugs.

The volunteers were amazing and need to be commended on their continued strength and energy. We left with a feeling that the future at Bratca is a bright one with the hope that volunteers will work alongside the Romanians to achieve a positive existence for the children. (Emma Wilkinson, Hayley Harper and Stewart Goss)

Not everyone who gave up spare time to visit Romania came to offer professional expertise. Some came to see for themselves the needy children and orphanages they had previously only supported from afar. Often these visits were a source of much general amusement, as well as providing contacts from home for the volunteers and new, exciting experiences for the children themselves. The Elastic Band, a group originally made up of students at a comprehensive school in Wadebridge, has performed at many White Cross Mission events, raising funds to support the care of the 'irrecuperables'. The group has since developed into an excellent and well-known band. They all took a trip to Romania to visit the places and people they had done so much to support. Two volunteers, Izzy and Juliet, describe the tumultuous effect their visit had on Bratca.

Saturday – market day, but this was no ordinary Saturday. Suddenly the normal Saturday morning bustle of the weekly shop was disrupted by bizarre Cornish notes floating over the heads of the Bratca shoppers and traders alike.

The woman on the second-hand clothes stall (with a bit of pig fat on the side to sell to those who have enough money for the luxury) perked up her ears and looked in the direction of the alien noises. Meanwhile the women selling goats cheese and overpriced eggs confused their calculations as they gossiped over what was going on.

Bratca had been invaded by more than twenty members of The Elastic Band, playing folk and lots of levellers music. Later on that day when the band played at Bratca Spital, the children who'd been with us at the market were almost singing along with the band – their first Romanian groupies.

As they played the children got more and more excited and as a few instruments were introduced for the kids themselves, the rhythms and tunes reached their pitch.

Then it was back to the apartment for boil-in-the-bag chile concarne (luxury for us poor volunteers) and Marmite on Bratca bakery bread (slightly different from your Tesco ready sliced and packaged brand!).

After that the instruments were collected together (and so were the musicians) ready for the onslaught on the Bratca Restaurant Bar. Many Bratca locals had turned up for the special event. The older kids who went along gradually mixed with the locals, strutting their Romanian-style barn dancing.

It was a great day – the kids loved it and so did we. Thanks guys.

8

The gift of giving

So far the story of the White Cross has concentrated on the people who have given time, expertise and practical assistance to the Mission, those who have been to Romania in person to help out directly. Other forms of giving have, of course, also been vital (and remain so) for the ongoing existence of the work. Without sponsorship and financial support, the Mission could not operate or hope to develop the care it offers to the children in the orphanages. Money as well as direct loving care helps keep alight the candle lit by the White Cross in the darkness. The majority of White Cross supporters are based in Cornwall, but now about 50 per cent of the volunteers come from other parts of the country, often having heard of the Mission through contacts at university or college. What is it that prompts people to give money or time to a cause which probably has no direct bearing on their own lives?

The psychology of giving can be complex, yet at its purest it is a simple and joyful impulse. There is such a thing as uncomplicated kindness which reacts spontaneously to the distress and needs of others. In his book *The Meaning of Gifts*, the Roman Catholic writer Paul Tournier gives a live example:

> This joy in giving develops more and more when the child lives in a harmonious atmosphere. I am in Algiers as I write these lines, having come here to see our grandchildren. The little girl is running back and forth from the house to the terrace from which I am holding out on this incomparably beautiful day. She is bringing me one by one all the pieces of her doll's dinner set; how much more pleasurable it is to multiply the presentation of gifts than it is to give them all at once! For the child neither social convention nor money nor ownership count; what does count is the heart-given impetus. He will give all that he finds. It is an act of regal love for him to pick a pretty flower in a public park and offer it to his mother. Why forbid him from doing this? Again, in the game of hide-and-seek, which children enjoy so much, they pretend to hide only for the pleasure of giving themselves away by coming out from their hiding places. The proof is in their happy outbursts accompanying their discovery after such a brief time of hiding! The supreme gift is the giving of oneself.

Happy are those who maintain throughout all of life this childlike spontaneity; happy are those who love to stand and look through the gift store's window or drink in the illustrated advertisements in the magazines – and are stirred inwardly as they think of all the wonderful presents they could give if they had the means.

The impulse to help others is natural and human, a marvellous gift from God to humanity. But the impulse to give freely to others is not so natural as to be inevitable or universal. Not everyone has that 'childlike spontaneity'. When we come across it, therefore, we cannot help admiring unselfish concern for others, devotion and self-sacrifice at whatever level. Rightly motivated giving is natural and good, and human goodness is universally respected. It warms the heart. The White Cross Mission warms many hearts because the spirit that inspires it is one of sincere compassion for the Romanian children – and its motive is to alleviate a tragedy and prevent further suffering.

It has been hugely successful in encouraging young, middle-aged and one or two even older persons to leave self behind, more or less, to travel to an unknown country and endure difficult conditions in order to care for some of the most vulnerable and traumatized children in Europe. The experience has for most been a discovery of the essential humanity which unites us all.

Pat herself gives abundantly of her time, energy and love. She is the person who created the whole project and who is still the driving force at the centre of it. She inspires all those who participate in any way, drawing her inspiration and her apparently endless reserves of energy from a firm faith in God and commitment to the spirit and teaching of Jesus. She is a dynamic representative of the Church which helps her in every way it can.

Yet this is not an exclusively 'Christian' mission. Christians and non-Christians work together without difficulty, absorbed in a common task, unconcerned about any differences of religion or philosophy. Their focus is wholly on the children. One knot of certainty which can unite all humanitarians, Christians and, indeed, the followers of any of the great religions, is the universal principle that we should do unto others as we wish them to do unto us. The parable of the good Samaritan (Luke 10:25–37) should arouse little objection in normal human beings of whatever creed or race. It was not told in praise of a Christian and indeed in the parable the follower of Jesus is told, 'Go and do thou likewise.' Genuine Christian faith should encourage love and service to others, which can be a great source of joy and vitality, as Wilfred Grenfell, the famous missionary to Labrador, witnessed:

Christ means to me the best kind of a Friend as
well as Leader, who is giving me in this world
ten times, nay the proverbial hundredfold as
good times as I could enjoy in any other way.

Genuine Christian faith should also prevent the slightest sense of superiority or exclusiveness in those prac-
tising neighbourliness and concern for others. The
parable of the leaven (Matthew 13:33) teaches that
yeast does its work best when it loses any individual
identity and disappears into that to which it gives
itself. So Christianity may achieve its finest influence
when it becomes anonymous and invisible as such.
'Humanitarianism' has universal acknowledgement
and acclaim and there is no debate about the value of
working to increase the health and happiness of others. To adapt the words of Rudyard Kipling once
more, it is 'simple service simply given to [our] own
kind in their common need'.

That is, no doubt, why some of the humanitarians
– and even some of the Christian humanitarians –
argue that dropping the word 'Mission' could improve
the charity's standing in the queue for donations and
grants; but although Pat, more than anyone, knows
how desperate is the need for money, she is determined that the Church should be seen by secular
society as relevant to the needs of the world and
not merely as an institution that stands back, aloof
and pious. 'How else is Christ seen but through his

followers?' she asks. 'Every action is Christ's. God hopes, dreams and acts through us. I want the Church and Christians to be seen as the channels of Christ in the world. So why should we not be seen to be doing something positive?' Thus she retains the word 'Mission'.

Pat wants to get across this image of the Church as active and involved to the Romanian people as well. 'Christianity' didn't come to an end in Communist Romania, as in neighbouring Albania, because the Orthodox Church collaborated with the regime. People did not dare to stay away from church, but on the whole worship was a ritual only. The collaborating church, despite the many genuine priests, generally preached what Pat described as a 'compromise gospel' (*The Church of England Newspaper*, Friday 21 October 1994). No church is perfect. Any church may be taken to task for its apparent weakness or failure in some areas. No church, however, will be the object of cynicism or criticism when it is actively caring for those in need. It is good to see the Church which Pat represents being so deeply involved in the attempt to rescue those tragic children in Romania, carrying with it many others who do not belong.

One is bound to wonder what hope there is that one day all churches – not only throughout Europe but throughout the world – will cease to settle for anything less than a truly Christian spirit of forgiveness, reconciliation and practical compassion.

The power of unity would then be theirs and they would have far more influence over those who hesitate to join them. The ecumenical movement has been evolving for a long time, but in recent years there seems to be a new dynamic evident, particularly in Europe itself, with statements of commitment to practical and combined action to help the needy. The White Cross Mission is just a small part of this movement.

No one asks those who help the White Cross Mission whether they are Christians or belong to a church (especially if he or she is the millionaire for whom Pat is always looking!). There are not many millionaires to spare in Cornwall, but people have responded magnificently to the appeals made on local radio and television and in the press. Peter Bromley, a Promotions Officer in the West Briton, is one of the Directors and oversees all the Mission's publicity. He has been to visit the orphanages and is full of enthusiasm, working tirelessly on behalf of the White Cross. A West Country TV programme called *Window To Life*, broadcast in January 1996 and presented by Ian Stirling, included film of Remeti and Bratca and produced a great response – and not only from the Cornish: the children were delighted to see themselves on television!

Many have given anonymously of both money or prayer. Pat has constantly repeated the urgent need for money in her letters to supporters. In contrast with some charities the White Cross Mission is doing it all on a shoestring, but Pat regularly expresses gratitude for every gift, however small. Always she has asked for the support of prayer as well as money.

Thank you for all you are doing. Your fund-raising, your collecting, your interest and your prayers make everything possible. May God bless you...

We desperately need money to set up these homes ... and we're asking you to do whatever you can to help...

God is working through each one of us. It is with our hands He reaches out and through our hearts that He loves and cares.

Thank you for being a part of this work. We couldn't do it without you...

We continue to need money coming in on a regular basis. Please everybody who reads this letter do a coffee morning or a sponsored parachute jump and keep us going...

So far no one can yet qualify to be first in the White Cross parachute jump records, but other daring challenges have sometimes been taken up on behalf of the Mission:

THE CHANCE OF A LIFETIME
Your chance to abseil down
Probus Church Tower
Saturday 21st September 1996
Details from Jeff Townsend

The great abseiling appeal raised £3,000 for White Cross Mission funds in one go.

Since 1991 so many acts of loving generosity have taken place, far too many to mention even a fraction of them here. Pat was amazed right from the start at the flood of donations and offers of help which immediately deluged the infant Mission. The first firm to supply men and materials for the initial maintenance convoy, E. Thomas Construction, have a permanent charity committee. They raised an astonishing £6,000 by means of a sponsored walk, raffle and car boot sale to cover their trip, gave two vehicles worth £1,000 each and supplied two drivers. Others gave just as freely for that first convoy, including the Royal Mail, which donated a post van (a West Briton driver gave up his holiday to drive it) and South West Water employees, who worked voluntarily to repair a tractor which they contributed. A mechanical engineer repaired one rotivator and gave another and horse boxes with drivers were also offered. A holiday camp gave four hundred blankets because it was changing its linen. Doctors gave sample drugs.

The story has remained the same over the years and activity in support of the White Cross has been non-stop, with efforts being made by groups and individuals of all ages. Concerts, fairs, sales, sponsored walks, bike rides, swims, silences … In addition to the most generous donations mentioned earlier, which have made it possible to purchase the houses, there have been many other examples of selfless giving. Supporters opened a White Cross Mission charity shop in St Austell which was followed later by a sister shop in Truro. An appeal in January 1994 for music tapes, videos and CDs to be used for therapeutic work with the children or for sale met with a great response. A Motor Cycle Action Group Rally took place on 23 April 1994. They rode from Penzance, Camborne, Redruth and Falmouth to Truro, collecting cash and equipment as they went. June 1995 even saw an episode of *Songs of Praise* at Redruth Rugby Ground. All the county's choirs were involved, as well as school choirs and brass bands, compered by Roger Royle. It was hoped that twenty thousand voices would be there and that twenty thousand people would pledge £1 a week for five years – enough to build a hospital to which all the children from the remaining orphanages in Romania could be transferred. The list of fundraising activities could go on without end.

The creation of the White Cross Mission was a spontaneous reaction to an emergency. Like any rescue it entailed immediate action and little thought of the long-term responsibility which might be involved. The realization of the nature and extent of this responsibility has now been dawning for some time. What does the future hold? What is next for the givers? Many other charities which rushed in to Romania with aid in the early days following the revolution have now withdrawn their volunteers, but the White Cross believe that there is still vital work to do and they intend to see their responsibilities right through to the end, to stay until the Romanians can run everything by themselves.

Until now the White Cross Mission has managed to cope with the task to which it committed itself in 1991 with the backing of locally raised finance, wonderful voluntary help and an enormous amount of goodwill, courage and faith. Ironically its success, ambitions and determination to do a 'proper job' now force the question: has it outgrown its role as an 'amateur' (though registered) charity with reliance only on voluntary finance? It might become more efficient, effective and far-reaching if it were to go professional, but would it then lose its personal loving touch? One of the characteristics of the White Cross Mission which has touched and benefited the children in so many ways is its informality – and its willingness to get its hands dirty.

The needs to be met are clear, but each comes with a price tag. The primary commitment is to complete the existing programme, i.e. to help the Romanians provide the most caring environment and the most secure future for all the children in the two orphanages. This means continuing to provide salaries for the 'educators', whose training also needs completion; employing an additional doctor at Bratca; and ensuring the self-sufficiency of the houses and the establishment of their small businesses. Pat reckons the cost of maintaining the existing programme would equal the interest on an investment of £250,000.

Not all the children could live in the pattern of family life offered by the houses. Some of them need special treatment and care and will need this for the rest of their lives. Josif, for example, might need to go to the blind school at Cluj, as he has lost his sight permanently.

Pat also dreams of establishing a hospital for children like Dinu and Patrika, an intelligent boy trapped in a body weakened by cerebral palsy. There are others equally frail. This is an expensive dream and the cost has not yet been precisely estimated.

Another dream which has not yet got off the ground, but is possibly beginning in an embryonic way, is to start a drop-in centre for the street children in Oradea. One of the Mission's own children, Josca, is already a street child and as he speaks good English and German he might be able to assist in some way. A group of theology students in Oradea would like to help run it and they are already doing what they can on their own to help the children. The project would involve buying a shop, flat or some other suitable premises. The children could come in for a hot drink or meal at night, have shelter and a sleeping bag or mattress, and be given breakfast in the morning. Members of the *Foundation Crucea Alba* are already interested in the idea but are not yet practically involved. The cost of setting the centre up and running it for a year would be about £40,000, and even if it were then handed over to the Romanians (unless they were able to accept full responsibility) it would still need the support of about £6,000 a year.

The White Cross Mission has the expertise and has now established a reputation for creating a loving and caring environment, which is also happy and informal, for deprived and damaged children. According to a report by Dr Oros at Oradea, 'Remeti is now recognized as the best "Sectille de Neuropsichiatrie Infantila" in the whole of Romania.'

It has obviously given and could continue to give valuable help to Romania (where there are still other children not yet reached who could benefit from it) and maybe to other areas in Europe, if not the world. It is unable, however, to offer such help without sound financial backing. To branch out safely into a wider field, Pat reckons, would need investments of £500,000, at today's rate of interest and inflation.

Even if she could find him (she is still searching!), it would be presumptuous to invite her millionaire to bequeath half his capital to benefit the plans at present only dreamed of by the White Cross. But looked at from another perspective, among the 60 million people in Britain today, are there 500 kind persons who would offer £1,000 if 499 others would, or 1,000 people who would give £500 each, and so on? It need not be much and there are many of us. The future of the White Cross Mission is in our hands.

The future is in our prayers also. If we believe in God we can all pray. Pat is convinced of the power of prayer. In her letters she has always requested and expressed gratitude for all the prayers which she knows are being offered up on behalf of the Mission. She is contemplating the creation of a 'Fellowship of Prayer'. 'We have a lot of individuals praying for us but if they were all part of a big network they themselves would get a fair bit of comfort out of this.' She sees such an idea as comparable to the way of the Franciscans, who undergird all their work with prayer.

Prayer and work can act together. Pat herself has spoken of an action being a prayer, and prayer often needs to be undergirded with action.

After all, prayer is speaking to a Lord who knows exactly what must be done.

And the Sons of Mary smile and are blessed …
They have cast their burden upon the Lord.

9

Those magnificent maintenance men – and women

And – the Lord He lays it on Martha's Sons.

None of the care provided over the years by the White Cross for the rescued 'irrecuperables', none of the developing facilities, the recently bought houses, or even the upkeep of the volunteers' accommodation, would have been possible without the help of the men and women who undertook the maintenance work. They were, and are still, truly 'Martha's sons' (and daughters – with my apologies to Rudyard Kipling), offering practical action to accompany the prayer.

From first to last the maintenance or 'convoy' volunteers have undergirded the whole ongoing programme of the Mission and given it an absolutely essential support structure. Like the childcare volunteers, they give up their holidays and find their own fares and accommodation. The record of their activities retells the story of the White Cross Mission from another perspective. It offers a glimpse of the enormous amount of effort which goes on behind the scenes of many charities and which often goes entirely unnoticed and unappreciated. The White Cross's band of magnificient maintenance men and women are far from being unappreciated: greeted with open arms whenever a new convoy of practical help arrives, they are loved in equal measure by the volunteers, the children and Pat Robson. Juliet Rowe called them 'bloomin' lovely!' and that just about sums them up. Everyone admits that the White Cross Mission would be nowhere without them.

In advance of the first big Easter convoy in 1991 went several plumbers and electricians. Not only did they undertake repairs in the Remeti Spital and instal an electricity supply for the new washing machines, but they also laid carpets. Pleased with their work, they soon began to wonder whether they had been wise to take so much time over the carpets. Carpets and incontinent children 'don't really mix well', as they commented later. It was obvious that there were woefully inadequate toilet facilities in the spital, and in any case many of the children were not yet trained to use a toilet: when not making a mess inside, they were using the ground outside, particularly behind the front entrance steps.

Jeff Townsend, who has been 'Big Chief' of the maintenance team almost from the beginning, did not meet Pat until the summer of 1991. Jeff is a Mechanical Services Design Engineer with Cornwall

County Council. His wife Jenny, who had already met Pat, introduced her to Jeff in the church tent at the 1991 Royal Cornwall Show. Pat told them what was needed in Romania and Jeff, having the expertise as well as a Christian spirit, went to Remeti, and is still going, widening his activities to assist other charities in Romania also. Within three weeks of that first meeting with Pat he had organized all the necessary materials and was on his way by air to meet Steve Bird and Stuart Renfree, two volunteers from the first convoy who were driving a lorry to Romania. Once at Remeti they set to and repaired the older toilets, or installed new ones. But their job was not yet done; they also had to teach the children how to use them: definitely the trickiest part of the whole project!

In October that year Jeff Townsend and Jeff Hocking, with David Wallace, were in Remeti again, installing showers and emergency lighting in the spital. Then they went to work in the 'English House' which was for the time being to be home to the child-care volunteers. The two Jeffs (to make it easier for the Romanians to differentiate between them, Jeff Hocking was known as 'Mister' Jeff, and Jeff Townsend as 'Sir' Jeff) were the first to enter the house and saw what looked like a black carpet. In fact it was a layer of dead flies covering the floor. Never ones to shun a dirty job, the men rapidly undertook some thorough scrubbing and cleaning to make the place habitable for the volunteers.

Their visit to the village school, where they improved the lighting and repaired the washbasins, was the first of many opportunities – none of which the maintenance teams missed – to establish good relations with the villagers.

In spite of all they had done so far, 'Sir' Jeff reckons that it was not until Easter 1992 that the first real maintenance convoy went out, and then the main task was the conversion of the old Communist Party rooms in the village into the White Cross School. The children were not allowed to attend the village school, but Pat and the rest of the planning team were determined to create alternative facilities for them, somewhere outside the orphanage itself. The old Party rooms were perfect: they were in the centre of the village and only two hundred yards from the orphanage.

The maintenance team dug an enormous hole and set a septic tank in place, plumbed in two toilets and washbasins, made extra rooms, provided electricity and heating, decorated, and fitted boards, cupboards and tables so that when they left everything was ready for the children to start school. Four fully trained Romanian infant teachers had been chosen to work in the school with thirty-five out of the sixty children at Remeti. A uniform of black v-necked jumpers embroidered with a white cross was created to make the children feel special.

During the same visit that second Easter, the Wood-house was officially handed over to the White Cross Mission and Sir Jeff met a village character, 'The Mad Axeman'. Was this some crazy giant of a man fero-ciously swinging an axe? Not quite. The Mad Axeman was, as Alan Woodburn recalls,

> ...a tiny, frail eighty-something-year-old with a senile piping voice who could hardly lift an axe, let alone wield it. But lift it he did, in the early days of the White Cross. He contested owner-ship of the Woodhouse – a complex business of intestacy and village feuds which had left the house in our hands, not his. When the first volunteers arrived he had barred their entry, brandishing the axe in a way that could have terrified no one.

The maintenance men arrived at the Woodhouse accompanied by the Mayor of Bulz (acting for the Mayor of Oradea), the police and journalists, ready for the official handing over of the property. They were startled to be met on the veranda by an old man waving an axe and blocking the doorway. Animated discussions followed, but confronted by both Mayor and policemen, the Axeman eventually and reluc-tantly unlocked the door.

At the beginning it was not just the Mad Axeman who resented the invasion of the village by the White

Cross Mission. Many of the villagers were suspicious of the volunteers, believing that the Romanian government was paying them good wages. They could not imagine that people from so far away would come and help them for free, and even give up holidays and income in doing so. They also looked askance at the children – many were obviously Gypsies, historically not a favourite race with many Romanians, and they were convinced that the children all had Aids or other infections. When one of the volunteers asked a villager why the White Cross was so resented, she said, 'Well you do so much for them and our children have so little.' But gradually, the villagers and the volunteers developed a mutual respect and affection, helped not a little by the extra practical help offered generously by the maintenance convoys.

One colourful character whom everyone met and came to love is Ilyana, the Mad Axeman's sister-in-law. To begin with her nickname was 'the wicked witch' but it was decided that, even said with affection, it was unkind, for she is a truly nice lady. She is extremely round and extremely short and she has quite openly befriended the volunteers at least partly for what she can get out of them. As soon as she sees one she frames her requests – for a pair of trainers, a pair of knickers or gloves, a jumper – something that she imagines is surplus. She reminds everyone of what it is she wants, and says with a nice smile, 'I want a pair of trainers – I'm size 40.' How many pairs of trainers she has is yet to be found out. In return she comes to the Woodhouse with milk and pancakes and anything else she has to offer. She had a drunken son who used to sit around and do nothing all day and who died a few years ago of sclerosis of the liver. She is still very sad about it.

When the maintenance men were putting in a cold water main from the road to the Woodhouse, they had to cross Ilyana's land. To save her from always hauling water from the spring, they installed a cold water standpipe for Ilyana at the same time, a gesture which was very much appreciated.

The conversion of the Communist Party rooms also required the installation of a new cold water supply from the road, so to benefit the village, a standpipe and tap were installed which could be used by several houses previously having to rely on a spring. The maintenance team stayed in a building behind the village school and a group of Young Farmers constructed a climbing frame and see-saw for everyone to use within the grounds of the school. Sadly this was destroyed by some locals who still did not understand that the White Cross wanted to help the village as well as the orphanage.

It was while the convoy was there over Easter 1992 that Dr Giles Romanez, the eye surgeon from Dorset (who originally helped Josif recover the sight in one eye until the tragic accident with the biro 'gun') came to perform a number of operations on the children.

To celebrate his visit and the success of his surgery a barbeque was held in his honour, at which he was presented with a plate full of fish eyes! Dr Giles had been 'found' in response to an appeal on Radio Cornwall. Taking with him an anaesthetist, a hospital matron and a theatre sister from Winterbourne Hospital in Dorset, he flew out to join the maintenance convoy. They used equipment loaned by Treliske Hospital in Truro, and they not only did what they could to correct the squints from which several children suffered (and which was often the reason why they were abandoned) but they tested the eyes of all the children.

While the eye team was there the convoy men cheerfully slept on the floor of the old school building, huddled round a stove. Undaunted by the primitive conditions, maintenance men Robbie Alberry and Gerald Rogers cooked amazing meals and were sustained by the remarkable substance known to the initiated as 'Tiger's Milk' (another name for *palinka*). One of them said to Pat that it had been the best two weeks of his whole life.

The next trip made on behalf of the White Cross Mission by Sir Jeff and his wife 'Lady' Jenny was a rather sombre one. They had to drive to Heathrow, in their old blue minibus, to meet all the volunteers who had returned temporarily to England after the abduction of Jahal de Meritens following his argument with Dr Oprea. They were particularly glad to greet their elder daughter Liz, who had been out in Romania when Jahal was kidnapped.

Later that year, when the volunteers had gone back to Romania, another two maintenance men, Doug Benetto and John Tonnelier, installed a bathroom at the Woodhouse. Things were becoming really civilized!

In December 1992 Sir Jeff went out to Romania once more, this time accompanied by Pat's son, Philip. Philip had his own boat-building and shipwright's business in Cornwall, but that winter orders were low and business was generally poor. Pat suggested he might like to go to Romania to help with the mending and replacement of broken windows. He stayed on, getting to know the children, learning Romanian and finding that his practical skills were increasingly in demand. He became the full-time maintenance man in Romania, cooperating closely with Sir Jeff and his team and preparing everything for whatever project Jeff planned next.

There was an emergency while they were there that winter, when one of the childcare volunteers at Bratca became seriously ill. Philip and Jeff had to play ambulance drivers, taking her to the hospital where the doctor in charge invited them both to look down the microscope and confirm his diagnosis of meningitis. With the wisdom of their years of experience in such matters, they agreed! Thankfully the patient did recover. Due to her illness, however, Philip had to take her place at Bratca and Sir Jeff had to drive back home to England alone, managing to get fined for speeding in Hungary.

A large group of maintenance volunteers visited Remeti during Easter 1993. One was Siobhan, who produced a video for her course at Falmouth College of Art as well as joining in with all the hard work. The main purpose of the visit was to decorate the interior of the spital and install a telephone in the village. In just nine days of frenzied activity the dining room and ten salons were painted and decorated, a dental unit and a new set of showers were installed in the spital and the telephone was installed in the village Post Office.

This time the villagers showed their pleasure at the sight of the maintenance convoy by inviting them to their houses for *palinka*. Jeff wrote, 'We also visited the church for the midnight service and joined in with our children and the village in walking around the church in a candlelit procession on the Orthodox Easter Sunday.'

Summer 1993 saw Jeff, Jenny and their younger daughter Louise – at twelve years old the youngest volunteer to date – again going on holiday to Remeti, bearing with them a special seat for the Salon 6 children with a foam cover made by John Kelly, one of the maintenance volunteers. They were all disappointed that the children preferred to eat the foam rather than sit on it, but Louise was in her element.

She got on extremely well with the mega-boisterous Bujorel and seemed to have some mystical hold over him, for he followed her round like a tame puppy, obeying her every command.

Easter 1994 – and another group of volunteers were working at Remeti, decorating and upgrading the workrooms and installing new doors. In September, Owen Jose and two engineers, Martin Opie and Tony Wherrie, put in two heating boilers. With winter rapidly approaching, these were essential since the dreaded construction company (a large and influential employer in the village) had cut off the heating supply to the spital. The incoming convoy carrying the boilers hit a major problem at the German-Austrian border, where two officers insisted that the vehicle was overloaded and forbade them to continue their journey until over a ton of materials had been shed. This had to be stored at a local farm and retrieved later, which caused some unnecessary delay to some of the essential work, although nothing defeated the maintenance men for long.

Over Easter 1995 the White Cross Mission managed to establish a link with Spital 6 in Oradea and sent some of its maintenance team to help out. The object of the first visit was to install showers and decorate the children's bedrooms. However, when Jeff and his colleague Ben Abbott arrived, they found that the Romanians had already half-completed the job, so they looked around for something else to do.

Rummaging around in a store they found kitchen cupboards and worktops and a large number of floor and wall tiles. They were interested to learn that they had been brought by a man called John Boast, who was later imprisoned for attempting to smuggle children out of the country. He had intended the Romanians to use them but they lacked the skill and equipment to do this, so the maintenance team set about it with enthusiasm. They installed the cupboards and worktops, laid the tiles in the kitchen servery and painted the walls. They also constructed a climbing frame in the grounds of the spital which Jenny and Dr Simone (a child psychiatrist) painted in the colours of the Romanian flag. The volunteers were overwhelmed by the hospitality they received in Oradea and were especially delighted with the surprise treat of an evening at the theatre.

In August 1995 the White Cross Mission lorry was off to Romania again, carrying tubings and fittings to construct a climbing frame at Remeti. The construction itself was a joint effort by Jeff, Charles, a childcare volunteer, and Radu Platon, Dr Monica Platon's son (Dr Monica is the doctor in charge of the Children's Unit of Spital 6 in Oradea). Painting it was also a corporate affair. Jenny, the master artist, was helped by Rita, Erika, Cornelia and Elena, the other children being kept at a distance by Erika's dulcet tones shrieking 'Go away! Go away!' The children made a great discovery during the building of the climbing frame: the pipes could be used as musical instruments and high whistles could be heard across the valley for some days.

The lorry was also carrying furniture destined for the first house, 'Casa Fericita'. In October that year Jeff, with the help of maintenance men Peter Hedger and John Brewer, installed a kitchen and bathroom at the Casa, and a water supply line between the new well and the house.

Philip Robson had been given the job of overseeing the digging of this new well. His first task had been to invite the well digger to come and settle a price. The seriousness of the assignment must have impressed him for that was the first and last time Philip saw him sober. He would go to pick him up in the morning only to realize that he was already far too drunk to be lowered down the well. So Philip had to go a little earlier and a little earlier each morning, hoping to get to him before the drink did. Frustratingly for Philip, his efforts made little difference and the whole problem caused such delays that the well took a number of months to dig.

Finally, however, the well was dug and the digger was paid his last instalment. He took his money and walked to a bar on the other side of the railway track to celebrate the fact that he had finished the job. He staggered home, crossed the line in front of a train and was killed. A sad ending to a troubled time after the problems with the well.

The Easter 1996 convoy became known as the 'blue paint convoy'. They had been asked to paint the corridors of Spital 6 in Oradea and Jenny Townsend, gazing lovingly into her husband's blue eyes, decided to choose a paint to match. She did not get it quite right, but even worse was the fact that the head nurse, Jenika, was alarmed that the colour would agitate the children! Perhaps she did not know that blue is a colour often used to calm disturbed patients in England. The special relaxation room for the Salon 6 children at Remeti also has peaceful blue walls. The paint brought by the convoy (there was so much left) was also used in the Intensive Care Unit of Spital 6's Adult Unit. No complaints there! New oxygen lines were also installed by the team.

At the same time another group was at Remeti, painting the schoolrooms, installing a toilet (the original ones having been vandalized) and a water heater in the White Cross school, servicing the heating boilers at the spital and installing a new water heater in the doctor's flat. October 1996 saw a small group of volunteers at Bratca installing new kitchen equipment and electrical cable there in preparation for the new incoming service. The work was never-ending.

Easter 1997 brought the largest maintenance convoy to date out to Romania: four vehicles and twenty-four volunteers. They were split into three groups. One was at House No. 2, 'Trandafir', at Deloreni, installing new cement floors and kitchen units and carrying out general repairs. They moved the existing kitchen window and started work on digging a septic tank. The second group (Owen Jose and his crew) installed a new heating boiler in the village school in Remeti which, like the spital, had had its heating cut off from the communal supply. It must have been icy cold in there during the winter. The third maintenance team painted one of the salons at the spital, then set to work redecorating the entire Woodhouse. It had been home to over four hundred childcare volunteers since 1992 and badly needed repainting. All of the existing plastic cold water supply pipes were replaced with new copper pipework, run within the building to prevent freezing.

That Easter convoy included one very special volunteer: Viorel Robson, who as a boy had been badly damaged in an attack by his father, and then had the terrifying task of removing the corpses of his friends at Cadea. He had been adopted by his beloved Mama Pat and went to live in England. Now seventeen years old, he had worked in a hotel over Christmas in order to raise his fare to Remeti. He had come back to Romania to help.

10

The heart of Europe

Viorel's story is a true one but it is also a parable. A boy who has been brutally treated by his father and his fatherland returns, in the spirit of those who have rescued and adopted him, to help. This is surely a parable for the churches, for everyone, certainly for Europe and Romania at a time when that country is in the queue for membership of the European Union.

The White Cross is a shining example of a mission inspired by a truly Christian spirit which is doing what it can to heal a terrible tragedy. This spirit of practical compassion and reconciliation must surely do something to prevent, or help to prevent, such tragedies in the future. It is certainly needed if the dream of a united Europe as expressed in the treaty of Rome is to be fully realized. We are, alas, still far from the ideal: witness not only what happened in Romania but only too recently in Yugoslavia also.

It might be expected that the churches should be the main promoters of this spirit, and to some extent they are. Look at the response of 'Christian' Europe to the needs of Romania. One might say that the whole of Europe has been represented there over the last seven or eight years. Not all the charities involved have been explicitly Christian, but this coming together to help in a common cause is the sort of European unity which cannot be disputed. The churches, however, are not as fully committed to the spirit of Jesus as they could – or should – be. They should be leading the way in showing practical compassion, but too often they have either supported a nationalistic or ethnic line or have stayed too silent and complacent in the face of evil.

The divisions between the churches, caused either by them being tied to one side or the other in a dispute or by their differences in belief and structure, weaken the spiritual force they could be if they worked together. If they spoke with one voice and were united in spirit there would be more hope for Europe and its countries. The following two statements are to be welcomed, therefore, and the hope is that what has been promised so recently will be implemented with all speed.

The Statement of Intent of New Europe was issued on 1 May 1997 and runs as follows:

Christian churches in Britain and other organisations with neither political party affiliations nor commercial ambitions have declared their commitment to an ever closer union among the peoples of Europe. The original vision of this union, as expressed in the preamble to the treaty of Rome, has faded.

Our purpose, as members of British churches and other organisations, is to rekindle enthusiasm and hope for that objective. We believe that our European continent with its rich diversity should be united in common enjoyment of lasting peace, liberty, security and prosperity, and should pursue its vocation in promoting the vision of humanity. This is the intent of NEW EUROPE.

The Second European Ecumenical Assembly was held in June 1997 at Graz in Austria and its theme was 'Reconciliation'. The statement from the Second Assembly refers back to that issued after the First Assembly held in Basel in 1989:

> The statement from Basel on justice, peace and the integrity of creation, that 'Europe is facing a cumulative series of interlocking problems which endanger human survival' has been vindicated; even the cruelties of war have returned leaving wounds still unhealed.

The participants later spoke of their hope for the future:

> We came to the Second European Ecumenical
> Assembly because we are believers and because
> we wish to live by God's gift of reconciliation.
> We came with the hope that, if we are guided in
> our daily lives, in the lives of our churches and
> the life of our continent, we will be fostering the
> unity of the Church and of humankind.

Giving and forgiving are the essence of reconciliation and are made easier when we can face our own inadequacies and faults and see them reflected in the suffering and pain of others.

It is clear from the history contained in chapter 1 of this book and summarized in Appendix B that not only the Communist but also the Western capitalist countries with their policies and wars contributed a great deal to the unsettlement and poverty of spirit in the country over which Ceaucescu ruled. The abandoned children are a result of these policies.

We are victims one of another. Our individual responsibility for that particular situation may be negligible, infinitesimal or even non-existent. In our heart of hearts, however, although affluence and distance may cushion us from the facts, we know that we live in a world where there are areas of great darkness with people silently crying out for help. We are all involved and we can all take action against the darkness.

If this seems too sombre a reality, and the weight of it too great, we can take courage from the example of the White Cross. Some charities are withdrawing from Romania, but the White Cross Mission has staying power and its strength is that it is prepared to get its hands dirty, to do what is necessary. While there are at least 120,000 children in orphanages across the country still needing help, the White Cross is committed to remain until the Romanians have either the will or the means to manage by themselves.

Whatever shadow may fall across our lives, or whatever darkness we encounter, we must not curse it. There is something we can do. The brightness of the candle lit by the White Cross Mission may show us the way.

Appendix A

Gazette articles

MOST DAYS YOU CAN COPE ... BUT OTHER DAYS ARE NOT SO EASY

by Graham Banks

On a trip to Bucuresti, to meet a doctor at the airport. The plane was late which meant I had to catch the late train back. During that late hour I walked around the dark streets surrounding the railway station. You see tall dark buildings in front of you, a shanty town of timber-built shops and food stalls with bright lights lighting up the streets like large glow worms. Cars go whizzing by, fruit sellers are busy, the smell of food being cooked and Coca Cola signs flashing in time to piped music. The hustle and bustle of people walking, talking, laughing and enjoying a joke or two.

As I wandered, killing time, I strolled to the back of the shops. I found crates, boxes and bags of rubbish. In the dim morning light something moved. I looked closer amid the filth to see a stirring; looking closer, a shape moves – a child sleeping in the rubbish, clothed in rags. Hands, feet and face covered in cuts and sores. Stop, look and listen, but what can I do? The more I look the more children I see, all the same, all dirty, bedraggled, unwanted and unloved. Should I stop the passers by, dressed in their shell suits – the new uniform of democracy – and show them what I see?

There is no answer in my head. As I continue to walk towards the station I can only think of Stefan; an orphan in Remeti. Found on the streets of Oradea he had no name, no age, no place to go. He was named Stefan by the Spital staff. He can say a few words: bird, water and the others? We don't understand his language. Traumatised in his young life his behaviour is aggressive and bizarre. The joy in his life comes from sessions in the playroom, running along the corridors of the Spital pinching food from the kitchen. Playing cars he shows his obsession with real cars – and there a change, in a real car Stefan grows into the most normal little boy you ever could see, bright inquisitive eyes, relaxed and content with life and his surroundings.

Life has given Stefan a difficult start and perhaps the damage done can never be fully repaired, but we shall continue towards bringing him joy with love and care. His problems are recognised, plans and programmes are actioned, and yet one is once again drawn to the reminder that here, on the streets of Bucuresti, nameless, faceless children sleep alone.

THE CHANGING FACE OF REMETI

by Naomi Packer

When we arrived at the beginning of September, summer was still with Remeti. The mountains green and lush clothed in mauve and white crocuses. During our stay we watched them gradually change through the seasons from dense greenery to the burning orange gold of autumn, and now bare of foliage, they are shrouded in the eerie early morning mist.

Ilyana, our colourful neighbour, has had new additions to her household in the form of piglets and a new calf born late one night. Her grapevine once heavy with fruit has now given up for winter, entangling her house with a net of bare branches.

The Spital has also seen changes, large and small. The constant change-over of volunteers, working with the children and most importantly the recent but long awaited departure of Viorel to England with his beloved Mama Pat. New perspex has replaced the broken windows ready for the harsh winter months and the Spital food once readily available for all strong stomached volunteers is now scarce and we are no longer welcomed to steaming bowls of *mamalega* for lunch.

The electricity has been as sporadic as the food, sometimes leaving the Spital rooms colder than the air outside. This has now been rectified amidst much tinkering and twiddling by volunteers and with thanks to Owen, the heating man, who came to Romania for the weekend bringing warmth to the Spital and its children.

The village cafe-cum-shop-cum-bar has furnished its shelves with new delights – chocolate and hazelnut spread and apricot croissants and thankfully, splinter free toilet paper has now appeared. The cost of local Ursus beer, a favourite amongst volunteers, has now risen and fallen with the local price war – Cafe versus Restaurant Bar.

Changes have also been apparent in the Woodhouse, there is a more relaxed atmosphere now that the stress and tension of the infamous Bucuresti concert is over, remaining only as a happy, hectic memory in the minds of both children and volunteers.

Boudoir lampshades, courtesy of a creative member of the household, have appeared in every bedroom to cover the bare light bulbs and are much coveted and admired by Ilyana; for whom one was dutifully made in exchange for a pair of her thick, hand knitted socks.

Tiger, the friendly, but flea ridden, Woodhouse cat has been 'lost' half way between Remeti and Bratca, however its fleas lived on here for a while thanks to the many mice who have made their homes behind the skirting boards and under the floor boards.

Changes in the village have been both gradual and abrupt, but all are for the good of its community and are welcomed by the locals and volunteers alike. We continue to watch with interest and eagerly await the further progress which is surely to come.

* * *

A MONTH AT BRATCA

by Chris Saunders

It began with our arrival in Bucharest dressed for cool Autumn days to find a soaring 30ºC. We should have known then that nothing would be as we had imagined.

By 11 a.m. the next day we were in rural Bratca, being introduced to the children at the Spital and settling into the apartment. Mark had unfortunately returned to England, so we were on our own. Saturday brought a visit from 'Mama Pat' and 'Episcopi Graham' (Bishop of St Germans) and an exciting evening of wedding festivities. Sunday was the day for the mass Baptism of the Spital children including Viorel and Cornel, the two gentle giants. We walked with the staff and children from the Spital to the Biserica, each child with at least one adult acting as sponsor. The church was hot and crowded and we stood in a circle holding melting candles and wilting flowers. The font, which looked like an upturned bell, was in the centre. Popa went around the circle, signing each child and naming them. He was joined by another priest and they anointed each child, not just on the forehead but on the cheeks, chin, neck and ears, using a small enamel cross. Then the actual baptism with water followed by a procession around the church. Finally each child had small snips taken from their hair (is Popa filling a mattress I wonder?) Now it was Bishop Graham's turn to speak, stressing that we were all part of God's family. His words were translated into Romanian by Vasile, the blessing was pronounced and we went out into the sunshine. Only one of the children had seemed to be at all distressed but I think we all felt a sense of relief when the children were safely back in the Spital and eating celebration cakes.

Our days were spent mainly with the Salon 4 children. With the threat of colder days coming, helped by Graham (Banks) and Dorina, we transformed one bedroom in the apartment into a playroom. It was wonderful to see the delight on the children's faces as they hurried down the path each day. All too soon my month was over. Rumours that the new Spital will open its doors in November seem pretty definite so by the time Margaret leaves in January the 'Nucet' children should be there. More volunteers needed for next year – I'll be there, God willing.

* * *

HORIA'S HAPPY BIRTHDAY

by Lizzie Allan

When I awoke on Thursday the 16th February one of the first things that registered in my mind was the fact that it was in fact 'La Multi Ani' for Horia. I'm sure I wasn't alone as since the day we had arrived, in the New Year, and apparently long before this, volunteers had been subjected to months of a daily countdown towards Horia's birthday.

We set off to the hospital expecting the boy himself to come steaming towards us in the true 'Bucuresti Train' style singing 'Long Live Horia!' But, NO. Outside the school he stood, dressed in his best clothes, clean shaven (thanks to Tig), acting every bit the seventeen year old man; no more the boy, not our Horia. A new air of maturity seemed to have descended on him – no more 'train to Bucuresti', or 'Avion'. In his own words – 'Happy Birthday; *nu gluma*, serious.'

In the afternoon Horia managed to squeeze a party at the Woodhouse into his tight schedule of celebrations! Having a party at the school and one in the hospital we deemed ourselves lucky to have the privilege of his appearance! Seven high spirited children invaded the Woodhouse for an hour and a half demanding chocolate, *suc*, apricot jelly and sandwiches. Our amply proportioned neighbour Ilyana (with matching appetite!) must have smelt the grub from across the garden, for she turned up just as we cracked into the jelly.

Even Ilyana couldn't match the appetite of Robbi though, I have never seen so much chocolate disappear so fast. All the children were fairly excitable and a food fight could have easily erupted, thankfully though Marin was there to calm the situation in his usual diplomatic manner. In the midst of the chaos Horia remained unusually civilised, smugly posing for pictures and occasionally announcing with pride that he was now seventeen and not in the least put off by Ioska boasting that he, of course, had been seventeen AGES AGO!

The highlight of it all was the cake. I'd only been able to find nine candles but Horia didn't seem to notice the difference as he blew them out and made a wish ... probably for more batteries for his keyboard. My fears that the cake would suffer for lack of ingredients – sunflower oil not butter, the wrong sugar and the fact that Graham made the icing ... sorry Graham ... were all proved wrong as the cake was wolfed down by everyone. Managed to wrestle a couple of slices back into the kitchen for the volunteers though.

Fortunately the consensus was that the food was '*Foarte bun*' and Horia's profuse 'Thank yous' were unnecessary – the smile said it all. So the Birthday Boy along with Marin, Rita, Robbi, Ioska, Clara and Erica returned to the Spital in time for dinner; all informing us of when it was their birthdays and whom they would be bringing to the Woodhouse. Apologies future volunteers!

* * *

FEELINGS FROM A FIRST TIME VOLUNTEER

by Sarah Whorne

I was told so much and yet so little. Nothing could prepare me for the beauty of the country I saw as I travelled towards Remeti, the miles of flat open country developing into mountains. I was unprepared for the overwhelming feelings I had as I first stepped into Salon 6 and the children surged towards me, climbed onto me. I felt helpless as I was scratched, hugged, hit, fought over. I was scared as I realised what I had volunteered to do especially as it seemed many of the people I was with knew the children and seemed so confident and self assured as they chatted about the kids and how they had changed since last year, the year before. Was I going to be able to cope and help these children? Would I ever learn their names? I was unprepared for the feelings of frustration as I strove to understand what the older children were trying to say to me as I knew little

Romanian. I was totally unprepared for the way each child would, in some way or other, win my heart over, how I would find them all adorable and loveable in some way and how attached I would grow to the children, the Spital, and the people of the Woodhouse.

As I look back I realize you cannot be prepared for these feelings in England, and you wouldn't want to be. You meet each Salon 6 child one to one in activities on the programme and get to know them. You realize you can cope with the children, that they are all individual children with their own personality and you learn which are mischievous, quiet and loud. Maria, a local who works at the White Cross school, came over and gave us Romanian lessons and you start to understand the children and converse with them.

Now when I go into Salon 6 or enter the Spital if all the children come towards me I don't feel scared or overwhelmed because I know them and I've learnt I can cope.

* * *

A POEM

by Jill Hamer

Leave me alone, just let me be
It is enough that you are you
and I am me
A look, a touch, a laugh, a smile
Just sit and stay with me awhile.

Lost in the past sometimes I cry,
Or drop my head and heave a sigh,
A weight so heavy on my heart
It makes me sad, sets me apart.

You cannot know what's in my mind,
So just be patient, still and kind,
There's so much I'd like to share,
To show you that I know you care.

My outstretched hand I place in yours,
A trust that opens many doors,
A chink of light – a special sign
Now I am yours and you are mine.

* * *

Christmas and New Year in Remeti

by Dawn Roberts

Having spent a month in Remeti in the summer of '94, Malc (my husband) and I were keen to return as soon as possible but never dreamt that we'd be lucky enough to spend Christmas there.

Christmas is for children, and as I thought of all the Christmases I've had, and all the ones these children have missed, I was determined to help make 1995 a Christmas that they would not forget. We were working alongside like-minded, and very committed volunteers who arranged discos, parties and the making of paper-chains. I have many happy memories so it is difficult to single out any particular one but I will certainly never forget the genuine pleasure displayed by Josif when he opened his little present to find a cassette – he was ecstatic and I dared not look at the other volunteers because, like me, they were struggling to hold back the tears.

On a lighter note, neither will I forget the day that Horia took me tobogganing. He promised me two things; we'd go '*foarte rapide*' (very fast) and I was a 'good volunteers' and therefore would not be going to hell. He certainly wasn't exaggerating his speed but I was considerably more cautious as I'm not quite ready to put his other promise to the test!

Carol singing on Christmas Eve, taking the children to church on Christmas Day, being made to feel so welcome in Marcel's bar on New Year's Eve, and climbing the mountain on New Year's Day are just a few more treasured memories.

I hope I did help to make it a memorable Christmas for the children because I know, for sure, it was one I'll never forget and every year, as I light my Romanian candle on Christmas Day, I'll think of Remeti.

* * *

A CHRISTMAS TALE IN REMETI

by Jan Chapman

On 16th December I left England to spend Christmas and the New Year in Romania. I arrived after an exhausting journey for my first taste of Remeti, although I had spent a few days in Bratca during the summer.

I was greeted by a very warm welcome from the residents of the Woodhouse; Claudine, Sam (bless you both) and Graham, and a much needed cup of coffee. After the second cup I, and two other volunteers who travelled with me, Dawn and Malc, went off to the Spital to meet the children. First we decided it would be polite to say a quick hello to Dr Marianna, who invited us into her flat and offered us a glass or two of *palinka* (the first of many during our stay). Warmed by the *palinka*, we went to say 'hello' to the children. I'm sure every volunteer has experienced the tremendous welcome given, all the hugs, cuddles as they clamber all over you and the kisses, especially from Remus who never stops.

There are so many moments during my stay that were magic, but one that particularly stands out in my mind was the White Cross School's Christmas concert. After Father Christmas (Mos Cracium), a grumpy old man with a stick in Romanian folklore, had arrived the children settled down to sing their carols and present their winter and Christmas poems. One by one, some of the children stood in front of Father Christmas and recited the poems they had learnt, some needed a bit of prompting, others gabbled but one in particular, Dana, stood up and in a loud deep voice, shouted her poem. After each recital we clapped and when they all had finished, Father Christmas gave each child a present of a note pad, crayons and sweets and their faces beamed.

In fact we could have been watching a nativity play anywhere in the UK, the only difference being there were no proud mums and dads watching, just volunteers with lumps in their throats and tears in their eyes, but with the same pride seeing their children performing. It was wonderful to have the privilege of being part of it.

APPENDIX B

Romania's past

Romania has a history of instability. Its boundaries have been continually redrawn and it has been inhabited by an amalgam of peoples who had to survive a constant and centuries-old flux of invasions, conflicts and political tensions. The land was rich in resources, but most of the peasants, the common people, remained abysmally poor.

When the First World War broke out Romania was ruled by Carol I. A prince of the German Hohenzollern-Sigmaringen family, he remained neutral, torn between the two sides. After his death in October 1914, his successor Ferdinand sided with the Entente in 1916, partly because his wife was half-British but mainly because he had been tempted by the bribe of Transylvania. This promise was upheld in 1918 and the Allied negotiators at the Paris Peace Conference also underwrote Romania's claims to wider territories.

Greater Romania had been born, but although it was greater in size, it was no stronger in terms of coherence or permanence. The mixture of so many different minorities, traditions and languages has always added to the disharmony and still does. During the period between the wars no leader or party was strong enough to bring together the disparate elements.

In 1918 Europe's old empires were falling apart and being replaced by a collection of independent states. All of them had liberal constitutions which allowed for parliamentary government, multi-party politics and free elections with full adult suffrage. During the 1920s, however, authoritarian trends and traditions, inherited from previous centuries, were back in fashion in Eastern Europe and political violence corrupted parliamentary government.

Romania did not escape this malaise. The German Carol II became king in June 1930 and he founded the Front of National Resistance as a means of promoting his own power. The National Peasant Party under Maniu were unsuccessful in their attempts to influence Carol and in 1939 the Nazi-Soviet pact heralded the dismemberment of Romania.

Meanwhile the Iron Guards, the militant wing of the 'League of the Archangel Michael', rose to prominence with their slogan 'One man, one acre'. They offered a powerful combination of nationalism and religion and became the most dynamic element in Romanian politics. They marched through the streets wearing green shirts, with little bags of bloodstained

Romanian soil round their necks, denouncing everything foreign and especially Jews. Their 'reverence' of
the soil symbolized their faith in the earth from which
Romanians were believed to derive their legendary
strength and whereby they themselves had become
'new men'. They embraced the Orthodox church,
which therefore supported them. One priest even
became a prefect of the Legion. They boasted that
theirs was the only political movement with religious
affiliation and this increased their support. They
opened their meetings with prayers and focused on
the ritual of Christ's passion and resurrection, but
developed a perverted theology involving 'political
crucifixion' and a 'cult of death'.

After his defeat in the Battle of Britain in 1940,
Hitler began Operation Barbarossa, the invasion of
Soviet Russia. Carol II was forced to side with Hitler
who further dismembered Romania.

A military dictatorship was set up in what
remained of Romania, with Antonescu at its head
until 1944. Carol fled, leaving his son Michael to
resume the throne. Meanwhile, in 1941, Romania
proclaimed a 'holy war' against Russia and Romanian
troops took part in the advance on Stalingrad. The
British government declared war on Romania in the
same year. Until the end of the war Communist political opponents (including Ceaucescu) were imprisoned
at Tirgu Jiu in Romania.

Romania had become a helpless pawn, buffeted this way and that in the wars between East and West. In similar fashion, its fate, together with that of its neighbours, was settled in a cavalier and careless way at a meeting between Stalin and Churchill in the Kremlin in October 1944. It was a meeting which dealt a blow to the hope of many Romanians that a democratic government might have a chance to rule under King Michael, now that Antonescu had gone. It was not to be.

According to Volume 7 of Churchill's *The Second World War*, he and Stalin carved up the Balkan cake between them and it was he who cut the first slice:

'Let us settle our affairs in the Balkans ... so far as Britain and Russia are concerned, how would it be for you to have 90% predominance in Romania, for us to have 90% of the say in Greece and go fifty-fifty in Yugoslavia?' While this was being translated I wrote on half a sheet of paper:

Romania
Russia 90%
The Others 10%

Greece
Great Britain 90% (in accord with USA)
Russia 10%

Yugoslavia 50-50%
Hungary 50-50%

Bulgaria
Russia 75%
The Others 25%

I pushed this across to Stalin who had by then heard the translation. There was a slight pause. Then he took a blue pencil and made a large tick upon it and passed it back to us. It was all settled in no more time than it takes to set it down. After this there was a long silence. The pencilled paper lay in the centre of the table. At length I said, 'Might it not be thought rather cynical if it seemed we had disposed of these issues so fateful to millions of people in such an offhand manner. Let us burn the paper.'

'No, you keep it,' said Stalin.

It was Churchill, then, who ceded Romania to the Soviet Union, not surprisingly with Stalin's acquiescence. But this was not the only act of which the West was guilty, as Edward Behr writes in *Kiss the Hand You Cannot Bite*:

The Stalin-Churchill deal over Romania was, however, only the first of many concessions that would place the East Europeans behind an 'Iron Curtain' for nearly half a century. In the long run ... Maniu, who had put his faith in the Allies, and Antonescu, who had put his faith in Germany, were equally betrayed. (pages 76–7)

Bibliography

Behr, Edward, *Kiss the Hand You Cannot Bite: The Rise and Fall of the Ceaucescus*, Hamish Hamilton, 1991

Rady, Martin, *Romania in Turmoil*, I B Tauris, 1992

Sweeney, John, *The Life and Evil Times of Nicolae Ceaucescu*, Hutchinson, 1991